The

Jump

Land Your Dream Job

Useful Business, Corporate, Sales, and Work-Life Insights

Mustafa Toga

PRAISE FOR THE JUMP:

"I can say with total confidence that it has opened my eyes and that I finished this book with a totally new understanding of the hiring process, but also with the sense that we should truly value what is important to us when making decisions, be it work related or not."

— *Ana Sofia Barros, Sales Account Executive*

"If your future is important to you, read and share this book."

— *Jason Swan, Vice President of Sales and Services at Revulytics*

"An outstanding resource for job seekers or those looking to manage their career progression most effectively. This book is loaded with practical insights and tips to help today's professional move forward and is written by a real-world professional who focuses every day on building world class teams, by helping young professionals advance. This is an excellent resource."

— *Leif O'Leary, CEO at Intralinks*

"I would recommend this book to both people in the beginning of their professional life, and also in the later stages. It helps you to look inside and understand what is important to you and how to grow and be happy through your career and personal life."

— *Stepan Kondratenko, Business Development Representative*

"The Jump is a timely book about the whole job search process. Mustafa Toga breaks it into meaningful parts and shares all the practical information that a job seeker needs. I think any young person who is in college can buy the book, read it, and follow it step by step to be more successful in this process. It even takes you through 'after finding the job' phase too. A very informative and helpful book indeed."

— *Ozlem Brooke Erol, Founder of YourBestLifeInc. and Purposeful Business, author of "Create a Life You Love", co-author of "From Hierarchy to High Performance", career coach, speaker, consultant*

"An interesting and easy-to-read yet profound book for anyone looking for a well-thought-out career counselling experience with tricks, tips and stories on the hiring process and other aspects of life. Recommended for every young and ambitious person, including myself!"

— *Felix Muckenfuß, Graduate Biologist and Entrepreneur*

Dedication

To Ömer and Aygönül Toga, my parents, who gave me everything.
And to Ela Yaren Toga, my daughter, to whom I hope I can give
everything.

CONTENTS

ACKNOWLEDGMENTS

Publishing a book has not been a one-man show. Yes, the main driver is the author. However, publishing is a long process and many people have helped me finish this book, and I would like to acknowledge their support.

Inspiration: My baby girl, Ela Yaren Toga. Her first birthday was my goal to write and finish this book so that I can give her a nice present.

In addition, Murat Tekdemir, a young professional with whom I had an interesting conversation, which somehow brought the idea of writing a book into play. And of course, my Catalan friends Ramon and co., from whom I learned a lot.

Beta testers: Murat Tekdemir, Stepan Kondratenko, Ana Sofia Barros, Francesco Domizio, Susen Schindler, Burak Ertürk, Felix Muckenfuss.

Cover, Layout and Illustrations: Maya Grünschloß

Proofreading: Lucy Lynch

Introduction: The Making of This Book

Certain things start rolling much faster than people can imagine. For example, here I am working on this book. How did it start? Here is a bit of back story:

Just before my summer break, I was approached by a university graduate in Barcelona who was interested in joining our company and in discussing current openings. As I was heading off on my vacation, I kindly asked this student if we could catch up when I got back. He agreed, and so on my return, we met for a coffee. This informal 'get-to-know-each-other' turned into a two-hour chat, and – as I had a young and eager job seeker in front of me – I told him about my experiences of the hiring process and the key high- and low-lights of interviewing hundreds of candidates over the last ten years.

There is a saying that my Catalan friends taught me:

"(Every man should) plant a tree, have a child, and write a book."

I had already done my duty to mother earth, and I have also recently just become a father to my beautiful daughter... Then, while running on the beach one day, I thought about the meeting with the young job seeker, and then of my Catalan friends' saying. Together they triggered the notion that it would be a good idea to record parts of this conversation on paper and share it with students and young professionals who are about to start their professional career.

The aim of this book is to break up the interview process into parts – a step-by-step guide – and link it to 'sales', giving insights for each step of the way in order to help you stand out from the crowd and land your dream job. You will acquire helpful tools on how to best prepare for your next job interview, and, in addition, once you obtain your job, I will share suggestions regarding what you can do in your early career to become successful and find your desired career path. Finally, I will address the topic of work and life balance and what else to consider in life that can make you even more successful and live a fulfilled and happy life.

About Me

My name is Mustafa Toga, but everybody knows me as Musti. I am a Senior Sales Director for a software company, with a focus on creating and cultivating a culture of a winning team and building a talent pool that is beneficial for both the employer and employees to further grow.

My expertise lies in hiring top talent, team building, demand generation, sales, pro-activeness and empathetic listening. I love to work with young talent and be the 'door opener' and trusted advisor throughout the early stage of their career. It gives me great satisfaction to see how young graduates start with little expertise in their career, yet with great passion and drive grow and blossom like a flower over time.

One of my biggest professional accomplishments was the transformation of our Inside Sales organisation to more of a Sales Academy program for young potential. Throughout this programme, our young potential team members build the foundation needed for a successful career in sales and other departments within our organisation. The team has expanded from seven to 60 team members over the last three years.

Without any doubt, my biggest personal accomplishment is becoming the father to a wonderful little baby girl. I am eager to be both her hero and clown at the same time! The last chapter of this book especially is dedicated to her. This is how I will coach and mentor my girl once she is old enough.

Another accomplishment of mine is this book, which is addressed to students and graduates and is aimed at helping and guiding job seekers through the interview process in order to land their dream job. Throughout the book, I will summarise all of my experiences from the last 20 years and offer some insights from the sales and the corporate world that I believe are also important to consider.

After having interviewed more than 500 candidates (so far) and given more than 100 young people the opportunity to start their career with us, I have collected many memories that I would like to share in order to help others be better prepared for their career beginnings.

I am always interested in progress and learning, as I understand that progress is the most crucial pillar of happiness. In addition, I love to practice sport as it helps me to balance my mind, body, and soul. I am also a big advocate of LinkedIn to build and establish a professional network and gain useful insights and meet interesting people. I kindly invite you to check out my LinkedIn profile, get connected, and ask me any type of career questions that you may have.

Before You Start

One great idea of the beta tester (reader) Felix Muckenfuss was to use QR codes instead of classic reference notes. Hence, I have implemented this innovative idea and hope you like it as much as I do, as it gives you a very comfortable and easy way to deep dive into certain topics and read more about it with only one scan. If you do not already have it, you might want to download a free QR code reader for your mobile device.

Chapter 1

—

Before

Travelling – the Best Investment to Sharpen Your Mind

During your days as a student, you will have plenty of time on your hands. The question is 'what to do with it?' And, moreover, 'where to invest it?'

It is hard for today's so-called 'millennials' to have goals and a clear plan to start their journey. Don't get me wrong, it is not because you are a millennial. Many of my friends, myself included in fact, faced the same issues when we were students twenty years ago. Naturally, it is due more to the lack of experience. So, it is crucial that you use your (free) time wisely whilst you are studying.

You might think now, 'Oh no – someone else who knows better than me about what to do with MY time'. Or perhaps something more along the lines of 'leave my free time alone. It's called FREE-time'. Here is the deal: the biggest piece of advice I can give you is to travel. Yes, you heard me right. Travel. Travel as much as you can and use the time between semester breaks to go abroad. Ideally alone. The best option?

Backpacking. The more you travel (alone), the more you place yourself out of your comfort zone. You will discover new cultures, new people, new perspectives and new insights for yourself, and you will sharpen your mind and build social competences by being frequently confronted with new and unexpected situations. On the one hand, this will help you build confidence, and on the other hand, it will strengthen your creativity.

Business life can be like sitting on a rollercoaster with your eyes closed. You never know if the next move is up or down, or left or right. There is a dynamic market that can influence the direction that a company goes. In today's competitive environment, companies have the pressure of always being up to speed and adapting themselves to (upcoming) waves – or even better – to create a competitive advantage by actually creating the next wave. By a 'wave', I mean a trend or the next innovation. As an example, twenty years ago, there were no 'smart' phones. Of course, we had mobile phones (I am not that old!); however, the purpose of the phone was to call one another or to send short messages by 'SMS'. That was pretty much it. Oops, I forgot to mention the famous 'Snake' game – so we also had some entertainment. 'Snake' was a game that came with the Nokia mobile phones, and Nokia held 22.9% of the biggest market share in 1998.[1]

Soon, more and more new waves would sweep across the digital shores, and in 2003, 3G networks

---

[1]

were rolled out across the globe and a new era of mobile phones was created: the smartphone.[2]

Today, companies such as Apple and Samsung are dominating the smartphone market. However, twenty years ago, you would not think of Apple or Samsung when you were about to buy a new mobile phone. Today, only around 1% of people buying a new smartphone consider a Nokia.[3]

My point here is to stress the importance for companies to constantly adjust their strategy and adapt their business to market needs. If not, they can end up like Nokia in the mobile phone business. Therefore, most companies continuously change strategy and develop new initiatives.

Let's describe the market dynamics as 'external' factors. There are also 'internal' factors: your new future colleagues. Some of them will be your peers, some of them your team lead or managers, and some of them will be your manager's boss. They also have their own agenda. Some will be supportive, some will be neutral, and a handful may make you feel as though they are sabotaging you throughout your career.

These internal and external factors can create a lot of uncertainty, which in turn is linked to stress. And stress makes people nervous. As human beings, we like to know what is going on. Not many people have the ability to stay calm and cool in any given situation.

---

[2]

[3]

However, if you travel, you can train yourself for this. Uncertainty and the unknown will not scare you as much and any changes are welcome, with you being able to see them as new opportunities. Having self-confidence and the ability to adapt quickly to new circumstances will help you to shine throughout your career. You will not experience challenges in making friends with your colleagues, and your outgoing personality will make you a very likable peer. You will have no problems with starting a conversation – even when talking to the big boss – and, of course, you will learn when to speak up and when it is better to remain quiet.

Photos of some of my old passport's pages.

A Semester Abroad, Erasmus & Similar Programmes

Another good option is to do a semester abroad. This will not only help you to build an international network of friends but also, depending on the country you go to, will ideally help you to learn a new language.

There are people currently adding, for example, Spanish as a language to their CV because they can say "una cerveza por favor", yet little else. However, there are also people who take the time to study in a Spanish-speaking country and develop a solid basic understanding of, and foundation in, the language. I have not brought this up simply because you can easily be caught out in an interview, which can lead you to an uncomfortable situation. I am highlighting it as it is an amazing opportunity to learn and foster your language skills. If you are lucky and know very early on in your life that you would like to live abroad – try to study there, if possible. This will also give you a good insight into what it means to live in that country and will certainly help you to make friends with locals.

Networking

Below is the usage of famous social media apps in the USA – based on the data of SimilarWeb, an online measurement company that offers customer insight into website traffic volume – which was released for June 2018:[4]

- Facebook – 58 minutes (on average per day)
- Instagram – 53 minutes
- Snapchat – 49.5 minutes

Do the maths yourself, and to these numbers add the daily consumption of YouTube, Netflix, TV, and video games.

My point is not to argue or to start a debate about how much media consumption per day is good or bad. Where I am going with this is to get you to think about how else you can spend your time while you are a student. I have already pointed out the benefits of travelling; so now let's look at other things that will be beneficial for the start of your career. One of those things is networking. Networking will help you to establish professional relationships. You can get first-hand insight from people working at a company or holding a position you admire. You can do a reality check to see if what you are assuming about a company or role is actually the reality. You should also keep in mind that your network can play a big role in landing your first internship or your first full-time job. It is interesting to note that most companies have something called a "referral programme". The employer is essentially encouraging employees to submit the CVs of suitable family members and

---

[4]

friends for open positions. To fill open positions is very time consuming and to make a good hire is equally difficult. Therefore, employers can pay up to several thousand euros to employees for successful referrals. It is actually a win-win situation. With this in mind, your network is also of interest to you, as you can potentially bring them additional money.

How do you network? This is also a journey of thousand miles that begins with a single step. Our first step is to review who we know. Do any of your friends already work? Can we utilise our parents, relatives, and neighbours? Does your university offer career support services? Do you get guest speakers from companies at your university? Are there any work-related posts or related magazines around your campus? Does your university organise recruitment days? Are there any events and job fairs in your city? There are many ideas, and most likely numerous others that I've not listed here.

The question is, do you already know which sector or what role you would like to make the step into with your internship? If so, you can be more specific when establishing your network. If you don't know – no worries! You will still have plenty of time to discover your passion and your field. Your approach to the above could be a more generic, broader one. It is more important that you take that first step.

We started this section of the book by talking about social media. As there was no argument about the time you spend on social media, it won't be controversial for me to tell you about the benefits of another social media channel: LinkedIn.

LinkedIn

LinkedIn is a business and employment-oriented service that is mainly used for professional networking. It is ideal for building connections, posting jobs or searching for them.

As of September 2018, LinkedIn had 575 million members in 200 countries, out of which more than 46 million members are students or recent college graduates.[5] If you do not belong to the 46 million students or recent graduates on LinkedIn, it is now time for you to create an account. LinkedIn has a powerful search tool where you can easily find people

---

[5]

in your city working for a company that you are interested in. You can also follow companies and join relevant groups. It will significantly help you with expanding your network and finding interesting people who are not shy to communicate and respond to your questions. Some people may even be happy to have a coffee where you can have an informal chat and find out useful information.

You should have a compelling profile page with all your relevant achievements and a professional picture to top it off – and by professional, I mean professional. A nice picture from your last nightclub visit, unfortunately, does not count. It will be the first impression your potential hiring manager will have of you, and you know how much the first impression counts. Ensure you invest €10 to €15 into having a professional picture taken, which you can also reuse for your CV. And don't be shy to smile!

If you go to job fairs, recruitment days or get to know someone who is already employed – add them to your LinkedIn network. Who knows, maybe one day they can be a useful resource for you.

Another great thing about LinkedIn is the job postings. You can actively search for internships and, of course, full-time positions. Based on your experience and the current role it will also show you relevant job openings. In some of the job advertisements, you can identify who posted it, and it is advisable to send a LinkedIn invitation and message to this person before you blindly send your CV to some "info@companyname.com" email address. Speaking of CVs, let's take a look at your curriculum vitae.

Your CV – the "Six-Second" Shot

While researching more information on curriculum vitae, I came across a statistic, which I found on Google, highlighting that recruiters spend on average only six seconds when screening the CV of an applicant.

Six seconds?! Let's take a look at what can happen in six seconds. On average, a person blinks 10 times per minute.[6] Yes, you heard me right; one blink every six seconds. In other words, we have the time of "one blink" to convince the recruiter to spend more time on our application. I am not suggesting you take the quoted statistics solely at face value, as I am not 100% sure about their accuracy. However, from my experience, it gives an interesting insight and reflects somewhat the reality. Sometimes it is helpful to put yourself in the shoes of others. Imagine a recruiter. They are receiving, on average, 250 resumes per job posting.[7] This means that the recruiter needs to separate the wheat from the chaff very quickly. From

---

[6]

[7]

the 250 applicants, only four to six will be called in for an interview and only one will get the job.[8]

Considering all the numbers and statistics provided here, I am sure you understand that there is only very limited time for you to convince the recruiter and hiring manager with your CV – and the competition is quite big. Google also provides many useful tips on how to write your CV along with suggested templates. You may also utilise your career service department of your university if applicable.

In a nutshell, all I can say is to keep it short – fit it to one page. Make sure it is well-organised and formatted and check for grammar and spelling mistakes. Include a professional picture on it. Highlight key information such as your name, current and previous role/title, and company including start and end date, education, language skills, and your hobbies.

- Name: on one occasion I met a candidate who actually forgot to put his name on the CV. Seriously? Yes, seriously. No comment.
- Current and previous roles: using keywords, highlight the experience you have so far that will be relevant for the role you are applying to. If you are applying for a sales role and have previous experience it is crucial that you highlight any key information such as "calling

---

[8]

customers", "following up on marketing leads", "working in the customer service department", "running specific sales campaigns".

- Education: be honest and only list schools, colleges and universities that you have successfully visited and completed. Certain companies do background checks and you do not want to end up with them realising that something you have claimed is not actually true.

- Languages: is it really great to list six to seven languages when you only have strength in two to three, with a minimum advance level? Is it worth listing certain languages where you can barely articulate more than three sentences as "basic skills"? I doubt it.

- Hobbies: if you are lucky, you may list a hobby that is the same as one belonging to hiring manager. Why? Because people like people who are like themselves! As an example, if you like doing Judo and your hiring manager is/was doing it too, they may find you more interesting. In addition, certain hobbies can give clues about your personality, i.e. if you list basketball, the hiring manager may think that you have a winning mentality, drive, and that you could be a good team player.

Internships

Nowadays there is a positive trend whereby most universities make it mandatory for the students to use one semester for their internship. Ideally, it allows you to have a great experience in a specific department where you can strive to start your career.

The days where interns were in charge of coffee, making copies or for internal post deliveries are over. Employers now understand the fresh energy and sharp young minds they get from interns and therefore most companies invest a lot of time and money into training them. This helps the employers to build a potential talent pool, use the internship period to select strong candidates, and of course, eliminate the ramp-up phase if they were to hire an intern as a full-time employee vs an external candidate. By the end of the internship, the intern would already how to use the internal systems, and would know the people and processes, which are all advantages compared to an external candidate. In addition, an internship programme offers the employer the chance to facilitate knowledge transfer from current employees and also enhance the overall team spirit as many employees also look to mentor young students and professionals.

The intern also has a lot of benefits. A good internship will provide knowledge and skills to be successful. It is usually a safe playground where you can try things out and employers even encourage you to bring your ideas to life and take risks. You have probably heard the famous quote from Denzel

Washington: "If you don't fail, you're not even trying." Hence, an internship also allows the intern to test the employer, as well as the field in which they undertake their internship. For example, if you do an internship in the sales department, you may find out that sales is absolutely the field you would like your career to progress in. Or not. However, as the sales department works closely with other departments such as the marketing department, finance department, and operations department, you will most likely have the chance to discover other roles that might be interesting for you.

If you are lucky you will get a mentor assigned to you. It is important that you get along well and that you observe and learn from your mentor. The key to your success is your humble being, your thirst for knowledge and your constant (weekly) interest in getting feedback. You need to know where you are at and feedback, positive and constructive, if given in the right way, can be very useful. You should also have a meeting with the department leader half-way through your internship. The department leader will very likely obtain feedback on your performance based on your peers' and mentor's review. Strong leaders have good observation skills. Keep this in mind and always strive to leave a positive impact on everyone you interact with. If you get a training session, do not take it for granted and make sure you are proactively participating in these sessions. Absorb all the knowledge that is transferred to you like a sponge. Immerse yourself in a challenging and fulfilling internship, and do not be afraid to ask for more tasks if you do not have enough work to do. An internship is not the place where you chill. It is the place where you shine.

Just keep in mind that there will be decisions made about your performance. The department leader will most likely ask your mentor or group leader about your performance and how you fit into the company. If you do excellent work your chances of being hired after your internship are very high. Any poor rating on your performance will make things hard for you to land a full-time job.

Last but not least, you are going to make a lot of professional connections that will be crucial for you to nourish and stay in contact with. Later, when your graduation comes closer, these contacts will be very useful for you when you are looking to land your dream job.

Job and Career Fairs

Many universities offer in-house events where they invite companies who are looking for interns. There are plenty of career fairs organised throughout the year in the city or the next biggest city you live in. A job fair is one of the greatest opportunities for students to find a suitable internship, establish a network, practice interviews and professional meetings, and start to create their personal brand. A great preparation and solid understanding of your interest should be the pillars to start this path.

Despite universities making a big effort to organise job events in-house, many students are not seeing and realising the opportunity or are not prepared well for it. The universities usually invite companies who are mainly looking for interns and currently have internship openings, and the universities often send the list of the attendee companies to the students in advance. This is a perfect chance to do your homework and check out the websites of those companies. Do your research and understand the field in which the companies are operating. Make a shortlist of the companies that are interesting to you and prioritise them. Based on this, concentrate your preparation only on those companies. It makes a huge difference if you go to the stand of all present companies at the fair with little preparation versus being fully prepared and approaching a handful of companies that are really interesting to you. The last one will help you to stand out from the crowd, which will increase your chances of being hired. With preparation I mean that you really spend enough time on the company's website or on Wikipedia to understand:

- The company's history
- Its core products/services and key initiatives
- Its core values
- Its competition
- The locations of where it is based
- Its financial information
- Any recent news related to the company

Understanding the Dynamics of a Job Fair

While a career fair has a similar set up to any other professional fairs there is a small yet important difference. At a regular fair, the attending companies are interested in dealing and doing business with you as an attendee. In other words, they are proactively trying to catch your attention and involve you in business discussions to position their products and services. Ultimately the companies want to make a deal/sale with you and therefore there is a natural competition between the participating companies. To better illustrate this scenario, think about the following: the companies are the "hunters" in terms of trying to catch a deal and the attendees are "farmers", trying to collect information.

At a job fair, the attending companies are obviously also interested in you; however, the dynamic changes slightly. Successful companies would like to hire promising students and invest in their future. It is now the attendee (you as a student) who needs to be proactive and shine against the competition (the other students). You need to make a great professional impression and lay the foundations. As mentioned earlier, preparation, research and why you think you are a good fit for the companies are the starting points.

Make sure you dress properly (check the dress code chapter in this book) when you go to the job fair and have a positive attitude. Smiling and being curious will help you to set the scene. It is likely that you will be quite nervous, which is absolutely fine and may even help you. The key is to listen well and go with the flow of the conversation. Of course, you probably already have something set in your mind and want to quickly go through it; however, ensure first that you bond well with the interviewer and connect with them on a personal level. Being interested in that person and smiling helps a lot. If you are too nervous you may want to start the job fair with companies that you are actually not interested in. This ideally prepares you a bit and takes away your nervousness.

While approaching the stand of the company that you are interested in, ensure to build eye contact with the interviewer and shake hands and introduce yourself before you sit. During the first seconds, check carefully what type of a person the interviewer is, and make sure you adapt yourself to their style. If they take the lead on asking questions, go with it and while answering the questions establish a personal connection. As well as being interested in the position and company, also be sure to show interest in the person who is interviewing you. Ask questions like "what is your role?", "how long have you been working for this company?", "what do you like the most?" to name a few.

It may be also the case where the interviewer does not take the lead but instead wants to see your proactiveness in how you start the conversation. A good starting point would be something along these lines:

Option 1: "I have checked your website and I am very interested in your products/business. If I understand correctly, your main focus currently is XYZ.[9] Is that a fair assumption? How is the business shaping up?"

Option 2: "If I understand correctly, you currently have openings in the field of ABC.[10] Is that the only opening/department you have located in this city or are there also other openings? I am asking as I am very much interested in [sales][11] and wanted to know if there are internship opportunities currently at your company?

I am repeating myself, but the key really is that you do proper research, be positive and eager. This will already help you a lot. Try also to adapt to the style of the interviewer. If they are direct – be direct. If they make jokes – make jokes. If they challenge you – accept the challenge and professionally overcome the test.

Just before writing this section, I had visited two job fairs within one week and therefore have very "fresh" feedback around my observations. At those two fairs, we had around 60 to 70 students approaching our stand. Roughly 80% to 90% of the students did not know who we were and did not do their homework, despite receiving the attendee list of the companies.

---

[9] XYZ = ensure you pick a topic that seems to be a current priority for the company. The company's website and a bit of research on the internet should provide you with a hot topic.

[10] ABC = most companies have a "career" section on their website where you can find current openings and filter by location. Check out what openings they have currently in the city you are interested in.

[11] Insert here the role that you like the most (if applicable).

As we like to challenge people, we confronted the students about why they did not prepare.We had excuses such as they were busy, had a birthday, were travelling, and more of this type of thing. This may all be true, however, if you want to land an internship you better be prepared and prioritise the time you have beforehand. If the companies are making an effort – you also need to do your part.

Many students did not even introduce themselves when they approached our stand, nor did they look to shake hands. This might be due to nerves, but this is etiquette and good manners, both of which are important at the beginning. Some students started the conversation with the sentence, "so, what do you offer?", which I think is an inappropriate question for the beginning of the conversation. Please do not underestimate the power of the first impression (there is a dedicated section for this topic). The first seconds and moments of the conversation, or even simply the eye contact, will determine the flow of the interview. Be sensitive and pay good attention right from the beginning.

Glassdoor, another world-leading job and recruiting site, released a survey in 2017 to find out what hiring decision makers think are the critical skills that a job candidate should have. Around 750 recruiters, hiring managers and other relevant people across the USA and UK were considered for this survey.[12] The outcome of this survey was that nine in ten (88%) of the survey participants agreed that "an informed candidate is a quality candidate". Only candidates who are well prepared, know more and self-select the positions that are right for them make it to the category "quality candidate". In addition, they make the hiring process a lot easier and smoother.

According to survey respondents, below is a description of an informed candidate, which is taken directly from the website of Glassdoor:

- They are prepared for the interview and ask pertinent questions
- They demonstrate the right experience
- They are knowledgeable about the job role

12

32

and the organisation's culture and values
- They are prepared so that they have the right expectations about compensation and benefits
- They are engaged in their job search
- They are relevant as they present a customised resume or cover letter
- They are more thoughtful about where they work

Put Yourself in Other's Shoes

If you google the idiom "put yourself in other's shoes" you will find the following definition:

> "Put yourself in one's shoes signifies, that you place yourself in others' situation and circumstances so that you can understand them better. ... That means we have to put ourselves in a person's situation so as to actually understand them and their feelings."

When I see that a candidate or a student is not prepared for the interview or lacks any demonstrable eagerness, after a while I ask them the following question:

> "Imagine, after you have successfully finished your university degree you open your own company and you want to grow and hire people. What would you like to see in the person who is applying?"

Instantly the candidates start to smile and shine, probably because they feel in power of the hiring. Buzzwords such as motivation, drive, able to do the job, energy, enthusiasm are flying across as an answer. As a follow-up question, I ask if they think that they are demonstrating these characteristics during our interview. While some become embarrassed, many realise the point I am trying to make. Are you doing your best in being and demonstrating the person you would like to hire? It is the same for the hiring manager or interviewer. They would love to see this characteristic in you as well. That essentially means putting yourself in others' shoes. Be the best version of yourself. Especially if you would expect this from others.

Deep Dive: the Hiring Process

At this point, it would be appropriate to understand the hiring process. Most companies have a certain hiring process that they rely on. It helps the companies to have standards that are relevant. For example, everybody involved uses the same reference points when measuring a candidate, and of course, a well-defined process is more efficient and gives room for continuous improvement. It can vary from company to company, however, fundamentally it contains the following steps:

Need

No need, no hire. How simple is that? Or did you ever go to the dentist without tooth pain or any previously planned treatment? Essentially, there must be a need. Either the company is expanding, it is creating a new role, or it needs to replace someone who has left, moved to another position or is about to retire.

You should understand from the recruitment person about which of these categories the position you are applying for falls into. It will give you a lot of information and then questions that you should further discuss with the hiring manager. If the reason for the hire is because the company wants to expand – we can assume that there are other people (your potential new team members) at the company doing this role. This is good to know as there will be people who are subject-matter experts and can help you get up to speed faster. They can support you in your open questions, train you, mentor you and guide you to your success. You may have similar benefits if the company is hiring to replace someone. It is interesting to know if the person who is making the position vacant is still around. This will help enormously on the knowledge and work transfer.

Finally, it can be that the company is hiring because it is creating a new role. In this case, you may have the flexibility and be able to create something from scratch as it did not exist before. You can very quickly make a huge impact if you are successful and become a subject-matter expert. The downside here could be how to measure yourself. If the company or the hiring manager does not have historical data or experience it will be hard to set realistic goals and key performance indicators.

Create a Requisition

Larger organisations have certain policies and approval procedures that need to be followed. There is normally one (software) system for all the relevant information, such as which department is hiring, where the budget comes from, who is/are the approvers, what kind of candidate is needed, salary impact and ideal start date.

It is normally the hiring manager or someone from the recruitment team who actually creates the requisition in the system (a.k.a. req.) with all the relevant people included. An approval process then starts. The finance department confirms that there is enough budget to hire, HR (Human Resources) confirms mainly as a formality, and someone from upper management and corporate level then confirms it is aligned with the strategy. Only after all approvals are in, the recruitment team then starts to actively work on this need to find the right candidate.

Sourcing

At this stage, the recruitment team works on finding relevant candidates and receiving resumes. If not available yet, a job description needs to be created and posted on job portals and social media such as LinkedIn, and sent to universities or head-hunters (if applicable, some companies rely on the support of external staffing firms or sourcing professionals to find a candidate). Generally, unless it is confidential, companies also make the open position internally visible with the hope for potential internal applicants and references.

Keeping globalisation in mind, it can be that the recruiter, the hiring manager, and the candidate are all in different places/countries. This makes it even harder for recruiters to find talents in countries that they may not be familiar with. Although the recruiter is responsible for the sourcing part, many proactive hiring managers support the process. After all, it is their team that is impacted and has the need. Once again, I want to stress how crucial it is for you to be networking. In the short-term, there may not be a fitting role for you. However, in the long run, sooner or later something will pop up, and you need to make sure you are positively in the mind of people.

Screening

As a reminder, there are typically around 250 applicants for an open position at larger organisations. It is during the screening phase that the recruiters are shortlisting the most relevant ones. The candidates who belong to that group are informed of next steps, starting normally with a screening interview.

If you made it so far, it is a good sign. You are shortlisted...on paper. The screening interview usually takes place via a phone call, which helps the recruiter to validate if the applicant has the right skills and qualifications needed to be a successful hire. Based on this call, the recruiter will then provide feedback on strengths, weaknesses, on points to watch out on and salary expectations, along with an overall impression that the recruiter has on the candidate. The recruiter will also provide feedback from the other candidates. It is then the hiring manager who decides if they want to continue with the candidate to the next step.

Hiring Manager

The next step is often a face-to-face in-person meeting in the company's facilities. It is also common that the hiring manager has a phone call first, and if the candidate convinced them, they invite the candidate to meet in person. The hiring manager wants to hear your life story. They want to understand if you are an interesting person and if they can work with and manage you. They will check if you fit into the existing team and if you bring diversity. The hiring manager wants to see if you truly understand the role and how exactly your previous experience will help you to be successful. Of course, they also want to see your motivation, your desire and your excitement in landing this job, and the true motivation for your application. They notice your body language and try to read your mind to find out more about you.

If you pass this stage, you are on the right track. Additional meetings or phone interviews with other (senior) managers, key stakeholders and HR will be scheduled as a next step. The hiring manager would like their impression to be backed up and therefore the candidate may talk to the hiring manager's manager or another senior manager.

Additionally, if the candidate would need to work for a specific market or country where the hiring manager is not familiar with the local language – they may ask someone internally to have an interview and double check the required language skills.

Finally, the candidate will have a more informal and relaxed interview with the HR leader. Topics here are along the following lines: "does the candidate fit in to the company culture?" and "does the candidate share the company values?"

Decision

Once all interviews have taken place, the hiring committee meets for debriefing. Usually, after each interview, the person who held the interview will capture feedback in a common/open folder that is visible to everyone included in the interview process. It is also common that people score the candidates. Based on the individual feedback, the hiring committee agrees who of the potential candidates was the best fit.

It can also be that the hiring committee is not always in agreement. Ultimately, it is the decision of the hiring manager to give the green light. Unless the discrepancy is a large one, the hiring manager decides and confirms their interest to hire the best suitable candidate.

Offer

Now is the time for the HR department to formally send out the job offer. It concludes with the basic and key information and usually has a deadline of validity.

It is common that the hiring manager would have already called the candidate with the positive news and also that the conditions of the job agreement were discussed and agreed upfront. In other words, on the written offer, there should not be any surprises. If it is the case, there is definitely a need for clarification before signing it.

Chapter 2

—

During

Before You Send out Your CV

After spending many days and weeks on searches and writing the perfect CV you are probably on fire to send it out. Patience and a strategic approach will certainly help to get you that interview, rather than blindly sending out your CV to many employers with no responses.

Your first aim should be that your CV stands out from the crowd and that you pass the screening phase and get invited to talk to the hiring manager. By now, I hope you understand that your CV needs to be spot on when it lands in the recruiters' and hiring managers' hands. Keep unrelated information out of your CV and make sure you "mirror" the job requirements you are applying for. Don't forget that your CV will have little time ("one-blink"!!) to impress. The reader should see immediately why you are the one best suited for this job. Needless to say, you and others will have checked your CV for grammar and spelling mistakes, and formatting also needs to be consistent.

I think to have a perfect CV should be the easiest part. Once again, there is an enormous amount of information and sample CVs on the internet, which you definitely should make use of.

I previously mentioned that it would make sense to have a strategic approach. What I mean by that is that we should ask ourselves "who do I know at the company I am applying to?". Remember, for certain roles there are referral bonuses. Someone working at the company who you ideally know would have a monetary interest in helping you to land the job. If you do not immediately know who works at that company you are applying to, do some research. Again, LinkedIn will most likely be the most suitable tool to start with.

Once you have identified someone working there you know it is crucial that you meet and sit down with this person to better understand the organisation, the team, the hiring manager and the position you are applying to. This will give you a tremendous amount of information and insight about how to prepare for the interviews. What type of person is the recruiter? What is their interest? The same goes for the hiring manager. Are they a tough person and what is their style? With style, I do not mean necessarily how they look or dress. I mean how they interact with people. Are they someone who talks a lot, jokes a lot, a more direct person, a more political person, etc?

This key information will help you to better adapt once you speak on the phone or sit in front of that person. In addition, it makes a lot of sense to check the profile of the hiring manager on LinkedIn. The more you know about them, the more connections you can make and have smart questions during the actual interview.

Finally, rather than sending your CV directly to the recruiting or to the provided email address for the position, I would strongly recommend you give it to the person you know. They will ensure that it is on top of the desk of the recruiter and help you to get a little bonus in terms of the consideration of your application.

If you do not know anyone at the company, LinkedIn is still the way for you to do your research. You can do a filter search, ideally putting the location and the title of the role you are applying for. This search result will probably show you a handful of people who may become your next team members and colleagues. The same rules and approach apply here as described above if you were to know someone.

The only hurdle is that you are approaching a stranger on LinkedIn. However, the whole idea of LinkedIn is to make professional connections and networking. There is no reason to be shy. Write a short and compelling message that you saw an interesting job advert and would like to know more about it. Either this person can help you or direct you to someone else willing to help. In addition, keep in mind that for the referral bonus you do not actually need to personally know the person you are referring. In other words, these people you do not know would also get a bonus if they pass your CV and you land the job.

Deep Dive: Sales

You have probably heard or read somewhere that you need to "sell" yourself during the interview process. While this might have a slight negative connotation, I strongly believe there are many similarities between selling a product and successfully passing the interview and landing your dream job.

With this, I do not mean that you arrogantly demonstrate how great you are. What I mean is that there is a correlation between a sales and interview process. Therefore, it makes sense to have a deeper look into sales and what we can take from the techniques that successful salespersons are applying. The common steps of the sales process are:

Prospecting

To position your services or product, you first need to have the right audience – your potential customers. The search that salespeople do in order to identify potential contacts is known as prospecting. Good salespeople have a very good understanding of their products and know well which type of companies would have the need for their services. Based on this, the salesperson performs a niche search with the result being the audience they want to go after to make the sales.

Bonding

You may have heard the following: "people like people like themselves" and "people tend to do business with people they know, like and trust." Bonding is a "psychological" approach to easily connect and build a relationship with your prospects. For instance, you can mirror the tone of voice and also the rate of speech. Here are two examples that should help you better understand what I mean:

Example 1: have you ever met a friend randomly on the street when you had had a very good day and were full of energy, but your friend was not (or vice versa)? You may have been full of enthusiasm and up for doing something spontaneous, yet the way (quiet and slow) your friend was talking actually lowered your energy. At that given moment, there was not a match in mood, which was easily transmitted by the voice and way of talking.

Example 2: have you ever received a phone call from a very bad salesperson who was in such a rush to literally bombard you with tons of words within a minute without a pause and breath whilst positioning their pitch and services? This is exactly the type of extreme case that happens if you do not perform bonding.

At this stage, you also need to listen. Actively listen. There is a difference between listening and actively listening. Listening is the physical process of hearing. While active listening is concentrating on what is said and really understanding it. Needless to say, if you have an active listener in front of you, you feel appreciated, important, understood and it gives you the sensation to open up further.

To summarise, bonding helps you to build a rapport with the opposite person who you are dealing with. You essentially adapt your way of talking and also your body language to match that of your counterpart. It enables smooth connection and communication as it allows people to be at ease and remove certain tension and nervousness.

Identifying Needs

Perhaps the most important step in sales is the so-called "need analysis". You can rush through it, but you will probably wonder at the end why you did not make the sale.

During this phase, it is all about asking the right questions, actively listening and making your potential customer feel that they have the control of the conversation while you are actually leading it. As long as you engage them and let them talk about their needs, you will gain key information in order to understand whether there is business that your product/service can address and whether it is worth the investment of time or not.

Today's computer giant IBM developed a sales qualification framework called BANT, which is easy to remember and gives a high-level overview of what key criteria need to be given to distinguish between a prospect and an actual opportunity to make sales. According to the guidance, an opportunity is considered validated if the prospect meets three out of four of the BANT items.

BANT stands for:

Budget	What is the prospect's budget?
Authority	Does the prospect have decision-making authority?
Need	What is the prospect's business need?
Time frame	By when will the prospect be implementing a solution?

These four criteria are not built on each other and are not so common that you can clarify all points and questions on your first call or meeting. Excellent salespeople dominate this phase well and take their time to identify the relevant information to be successful at the end and limit the chance of surprises.

Value Proposition

At this point, it is the turn of the salesperson to talk and demonstrate why their product/service is a perfect solution for the need of the prospect. If the salesperson listened well in the previous steps, they will gently unfold the value of their product and make it a perfect fit to solve the customers business issues.

The value proposition is not a marketing statement about how great your product is. Nor is it what the salesperson learned during in-house training about how to position certain features or functions of the product. Value is something good salespeople develop with the customer in each interaction. If you are able to create a value, the potential customer will see you as a consultant or trusted advisor rather than a pushy salesperson who is only interested in commission.

Manage Objections

During the selling process, prospects may express concern, doubts or hesitations. Objections can occur at a very early stage, such as "I am not interested" or "I do not have time", yet it can also happen in later stages when you, for instance, negotiate the deal – "this is too expensive" or "we cannot afford it".

Below-average sales representatives get panicked and jump directly on the objection to justify their position. This habit can result in the salesperson being perceived to be pushy and the prospects decide not to move on. Excellent salespeople have learnt that objections are part of the game and do not take the objections by the actual words said. They stay calm and relax and try to understand the underlying concern of what is said. It usually takes two to three questions to get to the root cause of the concern. A good strategy in objection handling is to politely reverse what is said.

Here is an example:

Prospect: "It is too expensive."
Salesperson: "I am glad you bring this up. When

you say too expensive what exactly do you mean?"

Prospect: "Well, we do not have any budget left for this year".

Salesperson: "I understand. What are you going to do to fix it or can the business problem wait until next year to be solved?"

Prospect: "Actually not. We have some other projects going on that are linked and based on this project. For the overall success, we need to fix this issue"

Salesperson: "Good point. Would you think it makes sense to make your upper management aware of this to prioritise the ongoing projects and eventually to secure budget?"

Of course, this conversation can move on as you want it to go. The point I am making here is very nicely summed up by Albert Einstein: "If I were given one hour to save the planet, I would spend 59 minutes defining the problem and one minute resolving it."

Closing Sales

After investing efforts to get to this stage, it is now time for salespeople to acquire the fruits of their labour. By now, the prospect should understand the value they get if they purchase the product or service. There might still be some areas of negotiating the conditions, and at this step, it is crucial that you distinguish between "interest" and "positions".

Position is what parties say they want.
Interest is why they want it.

The key to success is to focus on the interest. In addition, the salesperson needs to secure the decision that the prospect wants to move on. It is important to understand what the next steps are to finally close the deal.

Follow-Up

Upon what was agreed as a next step in the previous stage, it is wise to set up timelines. If you are about to sign the deal/contract, it is essential to have deadlines for that final step. Setting up a deadline, on the one hand, helps you to understand when to expect the result (this will help you to be patient) and on the other hand, it gives you the legitimacy to follow-up after the deadline passes.

Even if you successfully close the deal it is vital to follow up with the "now" customer to ensure the delivery was all smooth and the customer is satisfied. This is not only to maintain the relationship for further purchases but also for references it is fundamental to keep in touch.

The Recruiter

If you get in touch with the recruiter, keep in mind that you need to be formal. What applies in terms of grammar and proofreading for your CV is also relevant for any exchange with the recruiter or any other person involved with your future employer.

As mentioned earlier, recruiters are usually more easy-going; however, this does not make you best friends where you can be very informal. Respecting and adapting to the style of the recruiter will help you a lot.

If you have scheduled a call, ensure you are in a quiet environment. By quiet I mean absolutely quiet. I had a case once where one candidate was on the way to the supermarket while having the call scheduled with me. If you are disrespecting the time that is allocated to you it should not be a surprise when you do not get what you want.

Life is unpredictable and maybe for a very good reason, in which case you need to decline or postpone the call. If it is unavoidable that you are unable to take the call, then that is fine. In business life, it is common that calls are rescheduled; however, you need to inform the recruiter in a timely manner, as soon as you can, that you need to postpone. Ideally, you let them know the reason for it and suggest an alternative date or hour.

You need to handle the interview process like a successful salesperson would approach a prospect. You must know what you are dealing with and what the core business and potential new goals of the company are that you are applying to. Homework and research are half the battle when talking to recruiters. It won't be enough to browse the website of the company that you are applying to the day before the call. You need to know by heart why you want this role and why you think you are the best fit. You need clearly articulate what you did in the past that will make you very suitable for this position.

Enthusiasm, motivation, drive, and spirit are other important attributes that employers want to hear and see in you. If you do not bring this characteristic, you should ask yourself why you applied for this role in the first place if it does not excite you. The only reasonable explanation for me would be that you want to practice an interview process.

Indeed, an American employment-related search engine with the highest traffic amongst the job sites, lists on its website generic questions to consider in addition to specialised ones:[13]

- What experiences and skills make you a great candidate for this position?
- What has been your most meaningful work experience?

---

[13]

- What do you look for in an employer?
- What are your career goals, and how do you plan to achieve them?
- What qualities make you a team player?
- Describe a major workplace problem you've encountered and how you handled it.

You may also be confronted with more specific questions, such as:

- How would your previous colleagues or friends describe you?
- What are your strengths?
- What are your weaknesses?
- What are your salary expectations?
- Is there anyone we can use for a reference check?

We could continue this list for a long while.

Ultimately, it is your choice to be upfront and prepared for those type of questions. We are talking about landing your dream job. You may want to ask yourself what you are willing to invest in it. Bear in mind you may get one shot to land it.

Employers often purposefully put you under additional stress, during an already stressful interview. They want to see how you react and can handle pressure, because if you cannot handle this, the employer will ask themselves how you will handle angry customers and real business life. Obviously, you cannot know everything, and some questions will surprise you, or you may get an objection here and there. Remember the techniques that successful salespeople are using. Breathe, eye contact, have a friendly and smiling face, mirror body language, voice and speech rate. If you do not know something, be honest and say so rather than making something up.

It Is not One Way

It has become a trend that some companies include in their recruitment process a so-called "one-way" interview, which is a step where candidates respond to a list of questions via video to present themselves and their skills. However, the traditional interview where you talk to someone is not intended to be one-way. Be aware that the employer has a need – they need to hire a new employee.

Although you want the role, the employer is also interested in finding the right person. This is important to understand as this should balance out the power and control during the interview process. It is not a boxing match between a heavyweight and a lightweight. It is not David versus Goliath. Both parties are at eye level. You should see an interview as a professional business meeting where you position yourself and understand the interest. This also applies for the employer.

You should know your value, strengths and what you want and also "challenge" the employer. In other words, ask the relevant questions that are important to you. Let the recruiter validate the points that are unclear to you and verify that you understand the position correctly. In addition to the job-related questions, you should also ask other questions as it is an excellent opportunity to gain more insight into the whole interview process, providing you ask the right questions.

- Since when has this role been open?
- Is this a replacement position or a newly created role?
- How many candidates are you considering currently for this role?
- What are the next steps?
- What is the time frame? And by when are you going to make a decision?
- Is there anything you can tell me about the team?

- Is there anything you can tell me about the hiring manager?
- Why do you like to work for this company?

Non-Verbal Communication

You are probably familiar with the phrase "a picture is worth a thousand words". It points to the concept that a complex idea can be transmitted with just a single image, and this image conveys its meaning or essence more effectively than a description does.[14] Hence, this saying supports the importance of non-verbal communication. Based on UCLA professor Albert Mehrabian's research, there is a "7%-38%-55% Rule" of human communication. This percentage describes the contribution of a message's elements, which are:

- Spoken Words
- Tone of Voice
- Body Language

Now pause for a second and think about which of these components equals to which percentage of the "7%-38%-55% Rule".

I have done this exercise in many training sessions with my team members at work. Most people guess that "spoken words" make up 55%. If you have

---

[14]

guessed so too, then you underestimate the power of non-verbal communication.

According to Mehrabian's experiments, only 7% of the message received will be based on "spoken words", whereas 38% relates to "tone of voice" and 55% of messages obtained and processed by your brain are based on your body language. While this finding can sometimes mislead and be misinterpreted, Mehrabian indicates on his website that this equation only applies when a communicator is talking about their feeling and attitudes.[15] The below example can help to illustrate what Mehrabian is pointing out:

> **Verbal**: "I really love you"
> **Non-verbal**: has a one-tone voice, the person avoids eye-contact, looks anxious, has closed body language, etc.

It is more likely that the receiver will trust the predominant form of communication, which to Mehrabian's findings is the non-verbal impact of tone and body language, rather than the literal meaning of the words (7%).[16]

15

16

First Impression

Many thousands of years ago it was crucial for the survival of our ancestors to quickly (a few milliseconds!) decide if someone or a situation was a threat or not. Even though nowadays we do not find ourselves at constant risk, we inherited the ability to make quick judgments and shape our minds about people we just meet. First impressions are influenced by multiple factors such as age, race, culture, language, gender, physical appearance, accent, posture, voice, number of people present, and time allowed to process.[17]

Although it is quite a complex process, a Harvard Business School professor – Amy Cuddy, who has more than 15 years expertise in this field – scaled down the process into two basic criteria:

- Can I trust this person?
- Can I respect this person?

Based on this idea, people answer the above questions during an immediate first impression, which will set the stage for whether they like you and want to conduct business with you. Psychologists refer to these dimensions as warmth (trust) and competence (respect), and of course, you would like to be observed as having both.[18]

17

18

Amy Cuddy highlighted that especially in business situations, people tend to overweigh the competence part as more important. This can lead to people having more of a tendency to focus too much on their strengths. Think and relate it to our example of the salesperson. If a salesperson talks too much and keeps repeating how remarkable their product is, it will probably backfire, and they will lose creditability and most likely the deal. This tells us that first, we need to gain the trust rather than focus the conversation on our competencies. Warmth and trustworthiness are the greatest facilitators of trust. Therefore, the first few seconds, moments and minutes, can have a big impact on how the rest goes.

Your interview does not start when you are sitting in front of the recruiter or hiring manager. It starts on the way there. You never know if you are going to meet someone before you get there. Maybe in the cafeteria close to the office or in the company's building lift. I often introduce myself as an intern or even another candidate when I meet candidates waiting at the reception. I am interested to see if the person is only friendly to the hiring manager or also has a smile and a warm introduction towards an intern. One of our company leaders once told me that he would always ask the receptionist's opinion about the candidate too.

Make sure you also greet and, if possible, start a conversation upon your arrival with the receptionist, or anyone else you meet. Not only will it help you to bring your pulse down and reduce your nervousness, but it will also help everyone who encounters you to see you in a positive light.

In addition, you need to ensure that you are in a good mood when you go to the job interview. Your aura needs to send the signal that you are grateful for this opportunity and that you want the job. One candidate I interviewed was about to leave for the airport after the interview. He did not give me the signal that he was glad to be in my office and was probably doubting the whole time if he would make it to the airport on time for his flight. What is the point in scheduling an interview just hours before a flight? It could be that our recruiter suggested this time slot, however, you do not have to say yes to everything just because you really want the job. As a reminder, you probably have one shot. I wouldn't bet my chance on scheduling the meeting at an inappropriate time.

Another candidate arrived at the interview with very glassy eyes. It was around 10 am. I do not want to assume that the person was out until 4 am the night before; however, that was the impression. My point is that you should know when your energy is at its peak during the day and try to schedule the interview for around that time. Keeping in mind the regular office hours of 9 am to 6 pm.

Needless to say, it is not wise to party the night before and in turn have a hangover on the day of your interview.

What Else to Consider

The list below is additional tips and hints to polish your personal brand:

Smile: probably the most key physical indicator of warmth. Similar to bonding as a sales technique, a real, relaxed smile helps put others at ease and conveys a sense of calmness and confidence. Smiling can help to avoid a wrong answer.

As an example, nine years ago, when I was having interviews for my current employer, something very interesting happened that has influenced my professional behaviour – especially when I interview candidates. I had, in total, five phone interviews before the final invitation to meet the hiring manager in person. I was very excited to get this job, also because it included my move from rainy Dublin, Ireland to sunny Barcelona, Spain. The first four phone calls were quite smooth and painless. I was already very sure that I had the deal in my pocket before actually having the fifth and final phone interview. I remember the moments before that call very well. I had my big smile on and I was in a very good mood. I was in my element. However, right at the beginning of the call, the interviewer told me something along these lines:

> "Mr. Toga, thank you for your interest. I am not sure what you talked about with my other colleagues in your previous calls. But if I look at your CV I do not see any fit at all."

I was quite shocked and had not expected something like this to come at all. In milliseconds I saw my dream shatter, like a balloon bursting. Despite this shock, I remember how I actually answered. I took a pause and gently smiled into the phone. I kindly asked him if he could be more specific and why he thought that. We continued the conversation and I positioned my strengths and justified the moves I had made so far in my career. At the end of the call, the interviewer disclosed his secret and told me that he had actually only bluffed and wanted to see if I could "fight" when confronted with a challenge.

Years later, after becoming a manager myself, studying around this topic and gaining experience, I found out that this is actually a tool in the hiring kit of experienced managers. For the record – I was hired.

Eye contact: what smile is for warmth; eye contact is for trust. Building trust in business with your colleagues, partners, and clients is the key foundation for your success. In a job interview, maintaining steady eye contact will demonstrate your confidence and self-esteem. Ultimately, appropriate eye contact will help you to build trust and indicates your interest in the topic and person. "If your eyes in an interview are fidgety or continuously shifting back and forth, this can mean you are trying to conjure up an answer that you are not sure is the right one", states body language guru, Susan Constantine.

Note also that you do not do the other extreme, which is staring. Unlike eye contact, staring does not allow mutual non-verbal communication. Moreover, staring sends some sort of signal of dominance, resulting in the person who is being stared at feeling uncomfortable and looking away.[19] This is the last thing that you want the interviewer or business partner to feel.

Dress Code: I have to admit that luckily there is/was an evolution on work clothes over the last few decades. The style in business shifted from strict formal to now smart-casual. Suits and ties are becoming rarer.

However, that does not mean you can wear whatever you want to an interview. CareerBuilder – a global leader in human capital solutions – which helps companies target and attract great talent, did a survey in 2013, asking 2,201 hiring managers and human

---

[19]

resource professionals about the common mistakes that candidates make.

Here are the top five:[20]

1. Appearing disinterested – 55%
2. Dressing inappropriately – 53%
3. Appearing arrogant – 53%
4. Talking negatively about current/previous employers – 50%
5. Answering your phone or texting during the interview – 49%

Nobody is expecting that you are error-free during a job interview. Yet given the list above and the nature of the mistakes being easily avoidable – do something about it. A clean, neat and professional dress is your

---

[20]

best bet. If you are in doubt, check beforehand with the recruiter if there is a particular dress code at the company.

I once had a candidate with a white suit jacket at the interview. It takes some carefulness to wear white clothes. However, this gentleman had the back and shoulder part of his jacket covered in coffee stains. It was impossible not to see it, and thus the question is, why wear it? You are better off with a clean long sleeve button-down shirt than a dirty suit, and when I say button-down shirt you should remember that you are wearing it for a job interview, not a nightclub. I have also had cases where some candidates did not button their top two shirt buttons – with respect, I am not interested in your chest hair.

The female candidates that I have interviewed throughout my career knew how to dress well. The only comment I can make here is that sometimes less is more when it comes to makeup. Decent, simple, and clean makeup looks much better than too much of it, and I would advise lower heels. An interview is not a runway or red-carpet event.

As a side note, haircut, beard, clean shoes, perfume, makeup, and fingernails are part of the topic and should fit into your overall professional look.

Your Meeting/Interview with the Hiring Manager

Everything we have discussed so far is especially relevant for this moment. Now it's showtime. It is the "final" match. No matter how good you have performed so far you need to be at your peak performance and win this match. The hiring manager is ultimately the decision maker and this meeting has an enormous weighting on the overall Yes or No decision.

Phone Interview

If you are not located in the same city you will most likely first have a phone interview with the hiring manager. Remember the three elements of non-verbal communication? "Spoken Words", "Tone of Voice" and "Body Language". You may think because the hiring manager cannot see you, body language does not matter. Even if you communicate over the telephone, your body language will still reflect your mood and feelings. It happens unconsciously.

Breathing patterns especially play an important role and influence how words sound and are spoken. Try this simple exercise.

1.   Stand up, take a deep breath and say "Good morning. My name is Bond. James Bond." Do this three to four times.
2.   Sit down and relax into your chair so that your shoulders and chin are relaxed and say "Good morning. My name is Bond. James Bond."
3.   Remain seated but put your feet on a table or desk and look ahead and repeat again "Good morning. My name is Bond. James Bond."

Can you hear the difference in each exercise? I hope you do, and this simple exercise demonstrates that your body language will clearly make a difference to how you sound on the phone.

With that in mind, choose the posture for how you would like to take the phone call wisely. When I have important calls I usually stand up. Make sure that there is no background noise and the connection is very good. It can quickly get quite frustrating if the interviewer needs to repeat themselves due to the poor connection or noisy background. Ensure that from a technical standpoint the call will go smoothly, and sound quality is crystal clear.

If you think multitasking is a good thing to do while having your phone interview, go for it. At least you will cross something off your to-do list. It won't, however, be landing your dream job.

Jokes aside, you need to be very focused and demonstrate your true interest. You need to carefully listen to what is said and asked, and you also need to know when it is time for you to talk and answer. You can only do so when you are carefully concentrated and 100% present. You may be eager and cannot wait to impress in showing all that you can and have done so far. However, never talk over the interviewer. Let the person finish their sentence and even allow two or three seconds pause to ensure it is really your turn to talk.

Over the phone, it is harder to keep people's attention. The key to success during a phone interview is compact and clear answers. In many ways, you want to handle the phone interview as you would treat a face-to-face meeting in person. You should have your CV in front of you and prepare a list of answers to typical interview questions. Considering these questions are so common, hiring managers will expect you to be able to respond to them effortlessly and without hesitation.

Practice with your friends or family members. You can do it also on your own by reading the answers aloud. For the sake of minimising filler words, you could record yourself while practicing the interview. With filler words, I mean words you often insert into a sentence for no real reason. You may not even be aware of this, yet many people have one or two words they constantly use. Recording yourself on video may help to identify those words and help you to cut them out. In addition to these words, noises such as "ums" and "uhs" should also be eliminated.

We recently made a video to recap and highlight our activities and performance that was achieved over the last fiscal year. I had a slot of 30 seconds to give a message. I was very much surprised at how many times I used the word "really" in that short period of time. It really was a really big surprise!

Common Interview Questions

We don't need to reinvent the wheel to understand what potential questions may come up during the interview. You will find many examples of "top 10" or "top 20" common questions with answers online. The idea behind this is that you practice them to more effectively answer them. Here are a handful questions you may hear, with some comments:

Tell Me About Yourself?

This is one of the typical questions you may be asked at the beginning. The aim here is that the hiring manager wants to hear your life story. Who is this person in front of me? What motivates them? What is important for them? What are their goals? Try to come up with a good short story: where you grew up, your education, your interest, your past and current work experiences, your goals. If you have something funny to tell about yourself – do it. We discussed that smiling is important and helps to ease the conversation. Gifted people take this opportunity and link their life story to match to the position that they are applying for and its requirements.

Why Do You Want to Leave or Why Have You left Your Current or Last Job?

This question can be a tricky one if you have a temptation to blame others. To make it clear, badmouthing your previous employer is unprofessional. The interview is not the right time for it nor is your potential next employer the right person to talk about it with. However, you need to be honest and explain in a professional manner the reason why you are ready for a new challenge. This is so crucial as you can highlight what really matters for you and motivates you. It is also a signal for the hiring manager to identify if there is a match or not. You should not worry if you are in doubt about whether your values match that of the company, and it is important that you raise any concerns. Why? Because it is likely that you are leaving your current role for this very reason. What is the point in changing jobs and facing similar limitations or challenges? As an example: if you are leaving your job due to enablement, and learning and career development are important for you, you should communicate this. In addition, when it is your turn to ask questions, validate the points that are important for you. To continue this example, you may ask: "could you please explain to me the career path for this position?"

What Are Your Strengths?

This is another great opportunity to highlight your qualifications and skills, while you are perfectly matching it to the requirements of the role. Rather than giving short buzzwords as a response, explain them in a short story that highlights your strengths. Let's imagine that you are applying for a sales position and you have an outgoing personality, like to travel, can connect well with people and are naturally interested in others.

You shouldn't say: "my greatest strengths are that I can connect well with people, I like to travel, I am interested in others and I have an outgoing personality". A better version would be: "since I was a child I have loved to travel. I am very much interested in new cultures and anything else new, and it fascinates me to learn about and meet new people as I am generally interested in other people. Naturally, through travelling, I have become an outgoing person and can easily connect with strangers and build a common ground for small talk."

As a salesperson, you will obviously work very closely with people. So, it is your chance to match your personality and shine as a very good match. Look back to the sales discussion that we went through, this situation is similar to the "value proposition" step. It is your chance to demonstrate why you are a perfect fit, but without overselling yourself. For any other role, you need to understand what qualities directly correlate with the position that you are applying for and build your story around that.

What Are Your Weaknesses?

This one is usually the follow-up question to the previous one. It can be also used as a trap to see how you self-evaluate yourself. Perhaps the worst answer you can give is to say, "I don't know (have any)". Nobody is perfect. So, don't pretend to be nobody.

Rather, see it as an obstacle and how you can best handle it. For the previous question, we were looking for characteristics that can best fit the role; however, now for the weakness question we can do the opposite. Choose something that is not critical for the job and mention how you are working on improving your weakness. For instance, if you are applying for a marketing role you do not want to highlight the following skills as your weakness: analytical skills, data-driven, communication and strong public speaking, content creation, strong organisation, and event management skills and similar. You can say something like: "good question. Well, I tend to be a bit of a perfectionist". You may want to add some more authenticity into this response to sound more genuine.

Here are some options:

a) "Good question. Well, I tend to sometimes be a perfectionist. I want to finish tasks in an exceptional way, which occasionally leads to me working more than required on a topic. While I still love to do an excellent job, I have learned to better verify certain deadlines so as not to miss them and deliver the job on time."

b) "Sometimes, I have to rush to get things done because I am a little detail orientated and I have also been known to obsess easily about my work, but I have learnt to time my tasks. I am now in the position to manage my assignments better, so I am able to finish my work within the deadlines. In the process of my work life, I have learnt more strategic ways in order to acquire a greater understanding in general of the work environment. Nowadays I can adapt faster to new tasks and I think that I am now more proficient in meeting deadlines whilst ensuring not to undermine my accuracy at work."

c) "Sometimes I tend to take on too much responsibility, but I have learnt to work in a team and to share tasks and responsibilities amongst other team members. I think that helps the team to build a stronger work spirit and the transparency to communicate and to inform the team also helps to ensure a high quality of work. Furthermore, it eliminates the key main risk and the team is more flexible to adapt to a wide range of tasks."

Why Should We Pick You?

This question is also linked to the "value proposition" stage in sales. To best answer this question, you ideally qualify what type of person they are looking for, what the hiring manager is looking for in the new hire, and what the company culture is. Neither being shy nor humble will help you here. You need to be precise, confident, direct and to the point in your answer. Moreover, you need to actively listen throughout the conversation to feed back the responses they want to hear.

What Are Your Goals for the Future?

The intention of this question is to better understand your aim to stay with the company. Most employers will invest in your future and won't like you taking the next best offer, or worse, lose strong people to the competition. Although it is hard to sketch exactly your five- to ten-year plan, you should give some guidance on what you would like to achieve. If you know you want to become a manager – this is the time to bring it up: "once I master and gain all the necessary skills to be an exceptional individual contributor in this role, I would be very much interested in gaining new knowledge and taking on additional responsibilities. I would like to contribute as much value as possible to the company and at the same time grow as a professional. Leading a team could be one option for my career path". If you apply for a role in location A and the company has a location B that is very interesting for you – bring that up as your future goal: "I would see myself for the next two to three years in A and mastering this role. My mid- to long-term would be to see what opportunities I would have to work for this company in location B."

Some advice: as "future" is a very broad term you may want to split it into the following categories:

- Short term: 0-1 year
- Mid-term: 1-3 years
- Long term: + 3 years

Why Do You Want This Job?

On the one hand the answer to this question can feature your underlying motivation for why you want to join this company. On the other hand, it gives you the chance to flash and summarise what you know about the role and company and why you think you are the most suitable for this role. If you do it right. I often get answers such as "well, my partner moved to Barcelona and I am joining her move and looking for a new role". This might be true. But it is also true that you send red flag signals to the hiring manager. In other words, you are saying "I was actually not interested in moving here, but because my private life situation changed, I need a new job. Perhaps if my partner moves again next year to London I will follow her". Another classic response is "I really love the sun and the beach. And Barcelona is very famous for that." I am not suggesting you should lie; however, you need to truly demonstrate your motivation and why you are a perfect fit for this role.

How about this: "while I am quite young and flexible I want to capitalise on my freedom and gain international working experience. As I understand correctly, you have a very diverse team and I am eager to learn about new cultures and influence how other people think and try to solve problems. This will enrich my skills and help me to be more open-minded for new ideas. In addition, I really like to work hard and also pay attention to work-life balance. Your role in Barcelona seems to be a good compromise for having both."

Tell Me About a Situation Where You Needed to Overcome a Challenge?

With this question, the interviewer would like to check your decision-making skills, and also to some extent see if you have creativity in solving issues. You may want to think about one or two example that are adequate for this purpose and explain your justification and reason for your decisions or moves in order to meet the challenge.

What Is Your Salary Expectation?

I will dedicate a special section for negotiating the best salary later; however, for the purpose of completing the list of most common questions, I will quickly go through it. To make it simple: if you know the market and how much the job is worth, provide them a range. As an example, if the entry level for the position is €22.000 per year, give them a range like €21.000 to €26.000 as your expectation. Do this only if you are asked and if you are really knowledgeable about the market range. The phone interview is actually not the best place to talk about it. But again, if you are asked and if you know and have certain expectations, feel free to share them. It may also help you both to save time if your expectations are not met with the offer they can provide.

Tip: carefully choose the low end of the salary range in order not to miss an opportunity. If you are not sure about the standard salaries for this role, nicely objection handle this question with a smile and postpone for a later stage: "good point. At this stage, I am actually flexible and would like to better understand this great opportunity and also the career path and the overall package you offer your employees. Once I better understand those, I would be more comfortable to answer your question."

Do You Have Any Questions?

When the interviewer has a solid picture after grilling you with all the questions described above, they may ask as a final question "is there anything else you would like to know?" You are probably happy that the interview is almost over and cannot wait to go outside for some fresh air and to relax. But do not rush and spoil your turn. Bear in mind that this is not one way and appeal to your confidence that you also have a value. When I was a kid, our English school teacher would always say: "every man is the architect of his own fortune."

Back in those days, when I was young, I did not really understand what it meant. Now I am older, and I still do not understand it. Just kidding. My understanding of this saying now is that it is really in your hands regarding how you would like your future to go. You are responsible for the actions you take or do not take, which will determine your future.

To make the link to our topic, it is also in your hands to set the stage and pin down the flow of the interview conversation. You can ask at the early stage of the interview, when it is an appropriate time, how the interviewer prefers questions to be raised during the interview. Ask if it is OK to raise the questions during the conversation or would they prefer to keep them to the end. If they agree that you can ask questions while they speak, you have the permission to raise any questions and you have the chance to better qualify their words. You also ensure that the interview does not come across like a police officer questioning or examination, and instead it will feel like a professional conversation about the business.

If the interviewer wants you to hold back your questions for the end, it is also fine. You can make a funny comment like: "absolutely, no problem. I hope we will have enough time as I have many questions and am excited to get them answered." With that, you demonstrate once again your interest, that you are well-prepared and excited. Moreover, the interviewer commits to allowing you enough time to go through your points.

Questions You Should Ask the Hiring Manager

Have you ever made a big purchase blindly? Like a new TV, a new smartphone or a new car. Could you ever imagine making a big investment without really investigating the features and functions and other specialties? You probably wouldn't, right? Why? Because you do not want to make a bad investment. The similar principal goes for the job interview. You will invest a lot of time in your new role. Make sure it provides you with the return that you are after. To validate this point, you need to take the opportunity to ask questions.

I am usually the third person in the chain to interview people. Before me, the candidate would have talked to the recruiter and the hiring manager. Most of the time I hear: "um, I actually asked your colleagues a lot of questions and so do not have any further to ask". For me, this response is an invitation to ask and check the candidates understanding of the role.

Generally, I ask them:

- What do you think a typical day will look like for you?
- What are the key skills to be successful in this position?
- What do you think are the biggest challenges?
- What would your current employer say about you if I would call them for a reference?

If the candidate does not clearly answer the first three questions, I doubt I would give a thumbs up to the hiring manager to move forward. I cannot stress enough that you should have a sufficient amount of relevant questions to talk about with your potential new employer. Even if it means that you ask the same/similar question twice to different interviewers. Through your questions, you can confirm if the role and company is a good fit for your skills and expectations. Here is a list of suggested questions to ask the hiring manager:

Is This a Newly Created Role? Or Will I be Replacing Someone?

The answer to this question will help you to better understand the dynamics of the role. If it is a newly created role, it could be that the hiring manager does not have historical data to measure your work. It will be harder to compare your achievement and success to others; however, it also brings a great opportunity for you to create something from scratch and quickly become a subject-matter expert if you master it well. If you are replacing someone, it would be interesting to know why this person is no longer pursuing this role. Have they been promoted, changed department, resigned or been fired? If they have continued working at the company, it would be compelling to know if they will have time to transition their work. If they have left the company, understand the reason.

What Is a Typical Career Path for This Role?

With this, you demonstrate your eagerness to learn and grow with the employer. It shows that you are engaged and not joining the company to remain in the same position for a very long while. Even if it is a little early, it will give you a sense of how to build your milestones once you join the company. After you really understand the career path and have a concrete second role in mind, you can build that into your performance reviews, which you will probably have two to four times a year with your manager.

What Do You Expect from the New Hire in the First 90 Days?

Understanding the expectations and being aligned with your management team will be one of the strongest pillars of your success and growth within the company. For this to happen, you need to constantly (weekly) review your progress and get feedback from your direct report. It can be that you will go through an onboarding process during the first six weeks. It can also be that there is a huge amount of backlog work that needs to be done and you have a hybrid role. Partially onboarding and partially getting your hands straight in.

Will I Have a Mentor Assigned?

The response to this will highlight if you are getting support in your early stage or if you going to be a lone fighter. Do not worry if the employer does not have any official mentorship programme. There are usually enough willing employees who voluntarily offer their support. Your proactiveness is also required. If you need something, ask for it.

What Do You Like the Most at This Company?

This question will help you to build a personal connection with the hiring manager and may help you to identify what they like or appreciate the most.

What Would Be Your Suggestion to the New Hire on How to Be Successful in This Role?

Ideally, through the responses, you will find out how the hiring manager is measuring the work. You are probably also going to hear what they most care about and put the focus on.

Is There a Chance to Meet the Team?

This question will underline your overall interest and will give you the opportunity to meet your future colleagues. It can give you a sense of what type of team dynamic there is in place and what you are going to be up against. In addition, if you get the chance to talk to the team members, spend some time at their desk. Get a feeling for what the day-to-day job will look like. Whilst doing so, you may also validate certain critical things and get a sense of whether the employees are motivated or not. Think about TripAdvisor. One thing is how the restaurants or hotels are representing themselves, another thing is the feedback of the clients. The employees will probably give you more accurate feedback/information about the role and employer. Just be professional and careful in the way you talk to your potential new team. Most likely, the hiring manager will ask them for feedback after you leave the interview

How Is the Hiring Decision Typically Made?

Here you will get a feeling of who has the power. If you ask this question at a very early stage when you talk to the recruiter, for instance, you will be better prepared for each interview you will have. It is most common that the hiring manager has the ultimate decision. However, if the other interviewers are showing a red flag, it is likely that they will rethink their decision.

By When Will You Make the Final Decision?

Many candidates miss this point and wonder why they do not hear from the company for a while. Normally employers interview candidates when there is an immediate need, however, it could also be that they are looking to hire someone in a couple of months' time. You need to understand this point to better evaluate the situation. Will you be willing to wait a couple of months or does it make sense to find an employer who has an immediate need you can fill? It is up to you.

Do You Have the Budget Approved for This Role?

Similar to the previous question, the answer to this one will give you a sense by when you can expect a decision. Typically, employers only make the effort to recruit if they already have a budget approved. However, as the business world is dynamic, it can be that there is a current hiring freeze at the company. Under certain conditions (i.e. financial constraints) the employer may need to control the human capital cost and therefore freeze the spending of money on new hires. Additionally, the answer will give you a good insight regarding when it makes sense to follow up. As an example, if the hiring manager says that in two weeks they will make up their mind, you can follow up then if you do not hear anything from them by then.

Are There Any Other Candidates That You Are Talking to?

As in sales, it is better to know if you have any competition. You will also get the chance to understand how likely you are to get the job. Needless to say, it does not mean that you will get the job if you are the only applicant. However, it means something if you are competing against a handful candidates or a dozen. This question also works the other way, and you may be confronted with something similar with regards to you talking to other companies. Here are two ideas for how you can respond to it:

1. As I am really interested in your company and in this role, I am prioritising my focus and talking only to you. I know it is perhaps not wise to put all your eggs in one basket, however, this seems to be a great opportunity that I do not want to miss.

   This may be a naive answer; however, it gives the signal of honesty and loyalty. It shows your real interest in the company.

2. Actually, I am talking to two other companies, and I am currently at the final stages for both.

   They may ask which companies you are talking to. In a best-case scenario, you are talking to similar companies, or even their competition. If you are a strong candidate this information will give a signal to the hiring manager to hurry up and not lose you to the competitor. It is a good way to create urgency to act.

What Is the Next Step?

There are many business meetings with no clear next steps and calls to action. You essentially spend an hour or so but without an action to obtain the outcome. Think about the salesperson. They will spend a lot of time on prospects until they make a deal. It will actually take them many next steps to get the deal (if there is a fit). A good salesperson knows that and ensures the time spent is rewarded by a clear next step, which is, in other words, a commitment from the opposite side. If, for instance, the prospect is asking after the initial call for some more information and brochures, they are keen the send them. Under one condition: what will happen next once I send you the requested documents? Would it make sense to have a follow-up call in a week?

With these questions, the salesperson is opening a door for a follow-up. The same goes in an interview. You need to know what the next step is and clearly ask for it. I have had many candidates who actually leave the office without really knowing what will happen next. If you really want the job. Ask for it. Clearly say: "thank you, Mrs. Smith, for giving me this great opportunity. After seeing your team, talking to you and your colleagues, my motivation to join your team has increased even further. I really would like to have this job as I strongly believe it is a great opportunity for us both. Could you please let me know what the next step is?"

How Was the Interview?

One of my favourite questions I ask at the end of the interview is: "if you had the chance to turn back the time and redo this interview, would you change anything?" This gives me the chance to see how the candidate is self-reflecting and evaluating themselves. I also use this chance to give feedback if candidates are interested. There is no better opportunity to ask about your performance than during the interview and find out if there is a match or not. Seasoned managers and leaders are happy to share their feedback and opinion if they are asked. Take this opportunity as it is a tremendous chance to learn, especially if there is improvement feedback. If you do not ask for it and get a decline in the next days or so you will probably wonder why you did not make it.

If you ask at the end of the interview for the honest feedback from the hiring manager there is a potential for you to do it better in another interview. However, you need to be open to receive feedback. In particular, improvement feedback. And do not take it personally, rather as a chance to develop yourself. You may ask (again with a smile): "this question might be a bit tricky and I understand if you cannot answer it fully. However, I would be very much interested in how you see my candidature. Could you please let me know why you liked me? And more importantly, are there improvement areas?"

Below, you can find more questions that you might consider asking, which I won't explain any further:

- How big is the team?
- How many departments work in this location? And is there any collaboration between them?
- Is there any travel involved in this role?
- Would you like to receive any references (if you have someone)?
- What was the biggest achievement of this department in recent last years?
- Are there further growth plans for this department and your team?

Meeting the Hiring Manager in the Office

If you managed to convince the recruiter and the hiring manager on the phone, you will most likely be invited for a face-to-face in-house meeting at the office. It is not a must that it goes in this order. It might also be that you are invited straight after talking to the recruiter to meet the hiring manager directly face to face. If you already talked to the hiring manager on the phone, they now simply want to see and validate the points taken after the phone interview. Of course, they want to further examine your suitability for the team and check your professional manner. For you, it offers the opportunity to personally connect with the hiring manager and differentiate yourself from your competition, namely the other candidates. You should also emotionally connect with the hiring manager.

There are studies supporting the statement that people buy based on emotion and then justify with facts and logic. According to Harvard Business School professor, Gerald Zaltman, 95% of our purchase decisions take place unconsciously.[21] You essentially feed, through your questions and demonstrating your skills, the rational (facts and logic) part. Yet, if you miss connecting personally with the hiring manager (as with the recruiter) you lose a great opportunity that will ultimately play a big role during the decision-

---

[21]

making process (95% of purchase decisions are made unconsciously!).

You may have an excellent qualification; however, if you miss the chance to emotionally connect with the hiring manager and anyone else involved, your chances of being hired are low. Candidates who make the strongest emotional connection will win the race. The way to emotionally connect with someone is actually simple. Be genuinely interested in the other person. Everyone likes to talk about themselves. If you use this and let the other person talk about themselves whilst you actively listen, you will make the person like you. If you want deeper knowledge about this topic I strongly recommend you read following business book, which is a classic: "How to Win Friends and Influence People" by Dale Carnegie.

A good way to let people talk about themselves is to actively listen, pick up on what they say and ideally show emotions. This is a good indicator of your interest and passion. If, for example, the hiring manager talks somehow about their dog or cat, jump on this opportunity. Ask a couple of follow-up questions and you will see how their mood, tone of voice and body language will change, and you will see that you are on a good path towards making a good emotional connection.

If you go to the office of the hiring manager, observe the room and decoration. Are there any personal items? Any pictures of family members or pets? Any trophy, reward or excellence award? Build a conversation around it when the time is right. Let the person talk about their achievements and passion or interests.

Furthermore, you can check the profile of the interviewer on LinkedIn. I see many people checking my LinkedIn page before they come to the interview. Despite doing so, the majority of the candidates do not use the information they find on my public LinkedIn page. Sometimes I confront them with it. I ask them if they had checked my profile and why they are not using the information that they found. Please do not get me wrong, I am not upset if they do not praise my career or background. I just do not understand the point in making the effort (checking the profile) and then not using the information. A classic example is when I get German candidates who researched my page. I usually start the interview conversation in English and sometimes halfway through I switch to German. The candidates are very surprised and some of them do not even realise what just happened. I am actually German and studied in Bonn (the ex-capital of Germany). Those are some pieces of information that you can find on my LinkedIn profile and start to build a personal and emotional connection.

During the discussion around sales, I highlighted the step called "bonding". This is another important way to personally connect with the hiring manager. We have already talked about adopting your way of talking and also your body language to match that of the hiring manager. While every individual is unique, there are certain patterns and characteristics of the personality types of people. Some are detail oriented, precise and need clear goals set. Those people are valued for the quality of their work. Alternatively, some are very competitive, self-centred and self-confident. They tend to get immediate results and are ready for any challenge. Others are helpers, have a lot of patience and are team players. They are in favour of stability and taking a methodological approach. And there is also the type of outgoing and fun-minded personalities. They like to be liked and social recognition is key for them. This type of personality is people oriented and usually very enthusiastic.

There are different books and tools out there to assess your personality and measure your behavioural characteristics. One of them, which we actually use at my company for self-development, is DISC. The acronym stands for **D**ominance, **I**nducement, **S**ubmission, and **C**ompliance; however, there is also another version – **D**ominance, **I**nfluence, **S**teadiness, and **C**onscientiousness. DISC is based on the theory by psychologist William Moulton Marston and the assessment tool was developed through works of psychologist Walter Vernon Clarke.[22]

It would definitely be an interesting investment of your time to also assess your personality. There is plethora of material about this topic online, and here is the link to a website where you can do a free assessment:
https://institutesuccess.com/assessment/disc/

---

[22]

Coming back to our main topic, it will perhaps be hard to instantly observe and understand what type of personality the hiring manager has. That said, try to make the effort to match their style and adapt the way you answer depending on the hiring manager's type.

To summarise, it is crucial that you emotionally connect, that you demonstrate your strong desire, enthusiasm, and interest in this role, and ask relevant questions. With that, you would already make a big step towards getting the job.

One other important point, which many candidates miss, is to ask for the job. A typical example is that after the introduction and question and answer session, there is a hole. Sometimes I consciously create this gap. It is an emptiness of a few seconds where I want to see the candidates proactively asking for the job and the next step. I usually ask everything that I need to know. Let the candidate ask all their questions, and then at the end, I ask if they have any other questions. If they say no – I wait, which leads to the above described awkward situation.

The hiring manager is not mean or playing psychological games with you. They simply want to see your proactiveness in "closing" this deal. They want to hear that you want the job. Obviously, you should not ask "Will you hire me" or something similar. You should have a closing question that demonstrates your desire for the role whilst also providing you with some information about the next step. And ideally, through the answer, you gain a sense of how likely it is that you won the race and will get the job.

An example to make the deal is a question such as, "from what I understand, I really like the vision of your company and this role and would love to be part of your journey. I feel my experience and background would perfectly fit into it. Is there anything else you would like to know about me? I am very excited and would like to know what the next step is".

In a nutshell, here are the key pillars for how to convince the hiring manager and get the job:

- Dress to impress
- Emotionally connect with the hiring manager and anyone else involved
- Be kind, stay humble and smile
- Demonstrate enthusiasm and interest
- Demonstrate your value and perfect fit into the role and company
- Ask relevant questions
- Ask for the job/next step

Salary Expectations and Negotiations

Many salespeople fear to ask the clients/prospects if they have the budget to invest, and many candidates also feel uncomfortable to talk about the topic of salary. It is a tricky but very crucial subject, and the timing of which is also very important. If you have not been asked, at the very latest, before you pose a closing question on getting the job, you should actively ask what package they offer for the role. You should have a good understanding on the part of the salary that is fixed and (if applicable) which part is variable and linked to certain goals and objectives. If the compensation has a variable part, ask what the goals typically are and if other team members usually achieve them.

Moreover, you should do your homework and beforehand do some research on the market range for that type of role, which you can use as your data point. With that, you will see if the compensation is fair or much lower or higher compared to the average. It could also be that you will be asked during the first call from the recruiter or the hiring manager what your salary expectation is. Again, if you know the market average, provide them a range.

Are there any psychological tips you may use, or the employer is using? Yes, there are. Something called "anchoring". I am not saying that all employers would do so, however, there is an effect called anchoring that causes people to focus on the first available piece of information (the "anchor") given to them when making decisions.[23] In other words, the first number brought to the table significantly influences the outcome.

An example of this would be the following scenario: imagine you walk into a big electronic store to buy a TV. You encounter the salesperson in the TV section and tell them that you are looking to purchase a new TV. If the salesperson at the store is aware of the impact of anchoring they would show you the most expensive TV they have in the store. Let's say it costs €2,000. This first suggested price will set a benchmark and any other TV suggestion will make you feel that you are making a good deal. For instance, if

---

23

they then show you a TV costing €800 you will instinctively and instantly compare it to the more expensive one and will think that you are saving €1,200.

The following example demonstrates how to avoid the trap of anchoring. Let's analyse how bargaining is done in the Middle East or any other country where negotiating is part of the (business) culture. As this is part of the tradition, both opponents are usually consciously, but at times may be unconsciously, aware of the anchor effect. Both parties start negotiating with two extreme opposite positions – one is asking for $30 for the product or service whilst the other is offering $3. The seller says, "my final offer is $27" and the buyer responds, "I can only pay $5". This then goes on with last offers and final last offers and they then find a compromise, or not.

My father is very good at this. When I was young we often went to the bazaar and it was always showtime to see my father in action. He is excellent, and if someone was asking for a ridiculously high price he did not hesitate to counter with a ridiculously low price. I witnessed deals that started at $100 and ended at $15 to $20. I am sorry if I just ruined your illusion of the last great bargain you made on your vacation! Now, as you are aware of this principle, you may also use it in your salary discussions, and if you combine it with a joke, you are more likely to get a better offer.

Todd Thorsteinson, a psychology professor at the University of Idaho, conducted a study examining this exact topic. In other words, what happens if you initiate salary discussions with an extreme request. In this study, 200 college students were playing the role of a hiring manager to find a candidate for the role of an administrative assistant. Some participants knew the candidate's past salary ($29,000), while others were told to ask the applicant what salary expectations they had.

Half of the time, the candidate jokingly replied with an insanely high anchor: "I'd like $100,000, but really, I'm looking for something fair." Other candidates replied with an unrealistically low anchor: "I'd work for $1, but really, I'm looking for something that is fair." Given that the candidate was a good fit for the job, the hiring managers provided a salary offer. The findings revealed that the candidates who joked about earning $100,000 were offered, on average, $3,000 more than the other group.

"Incorporating a joking comment about implausible salary expectations may be a relatively easy way for job candidates to establish a high anchor and minimise negative reactions from employers", Thorsteinson wrote in the Journal of Applied Social Psychology.[24]

24

Another Perspective for Salary Discussions

I do not want to confuse you with the anchor effect, nor am I suggesting that you must use it. However, I think it is worth sharing it here as it could be helpful for you (not only when you talk about salary).

You also need to understand that most companies are smart and pay enough money to attract and retain the best candidates. After all, companies have a different package for different levels. If you are coming straight from college with very limited working experience, they will offer you an entry package. This should be standard in line with other new employees who have recently started, for obviously companies do not want employees to feel that they are underpaid compared to their peers, which can quickly lead to a very frustrating team climate.

In addition, companies aim to build on strong candidates and are usually interested in offering a competitive package to get them on board and offer them a career path. Another good indicator that an employer genuinely values their employees are benefits on top of the salary, a few of which include restaurant vouchers, private insurance, birthday day off, flexible working hours, free tickets to events, free learning courses, and most importantly, a great team and culture. While it is, of course, great to earn a lot of money, there are other factors that will determine if your job is a dream job or not.

Lastly, before the interview starts, you should have a clear idea in your mind about the minimum salary that you are aiming for. As long as this is based on realistic figures (market search) and as long as you understand your value (minimum acceptable salary) you will be in a better position to negotiate and find a compromise. Do not be afraid not to go lower than your realistic expectation, and ideally you have some other options you can demonstrate. Something along the following lines will underline your interest in joining the company for a good salary:

"I am also talking to a few other companies, of which the salary is around the X€ mark. However, talking to you and getting a better understanding of your company's mission, I am very impressed, and strongly feel that I am a good match. Because finding the right role and a clear career path is more important to me than the money, I would be willing to accept something around the Y€ mark as a minimum."

Chapter 3

–

After

When you ask for the job and what the next step is as part of your closing question, you will probably get a sense of when you can expect to hear the final decision.

If you get an answer such as "we will get back to you soon" try to understand what "soon" means, and whether this means a few days or a few weeks. Moreover, be curious to understand if they are evaluating other candidates or waiting to get the final confirmation on the budget in order to be able to hire the right candidate. You can sit down and respect the deadline until you hear something from them. Or you can be proactive and do something.

For your own learning, immediately after the final interview, go to a nice coffee shop, review the interview and do a self-evaluation. Note down the things that you think you did well or received positive feedback on, and then write down the situations or questions where you felt uncomfortable or did not know what to say.

Were there any promises made? Was there anything you wanted to ask but did not have the chance to do so? Do you still remember all the names and roles of the people you talked to and did they give any useful information? Is this the company you have always wanted to work for? What excites you the most about this job? This information might be relevant for later and also helpful for the follow-up email you should consider writing to the hiring manager.

Follow-Up with the Hiring Manager

It is a small gesture, yet 99% of candidates are not doing it. You will probably only need to dedicate ten minutes of your time to it, and it really makes a difference compared to the other 99%. It does not need to be something complex. Follow the KISS rule. **K**eep **I**t **S**hort and **S**imple. An example:

Hi [Interviewer Name],

It was a pleasure meeting you and thank you for explaining to me more about the position, your company and introducing me to the team.

I'm very excited about the opportunity to join your team, especially due to [insert the main reason why you are excited].

Please let me know if I can provide additional information. I look forward to hearing from you.

Best regards,
[Your Name]

Connect with Your Interviewer Online and Notify Your References

If you have not already done so before the interview, make sure that after the interview you connect on LinkedIn with all the people that you met during the interview process. Ideally, you get the first job you applied for. If you do not get the current position, these connections are important if something might arise later. The recruiters or hiring managers usually also proactively use LinkedIn to post and publish current openings. This will be a nice alert for you.

If you gave references to your potential next employer, ensure you call your references to give them a heads up. You do not want your references to receive a surprise call. You may think this is so obvious. You are right. Still, something similar actually happened to me in 2008. Throughout my studies, I worked for many years as a waiter and barkeeper in various restaurants. Everybody knew me by my nickname – "Musti" – including the restaurant owner. When I applied for my first job, the company asked me to provide some references, and so I gave the contact details of the restaurant manager. A day later, I told him about it and mentioned that it would be likely that someone would call him about me and ask questions about my performance at work. Three weeks later, someone actually called him. Here is how the conversation went:

Reference Checker (RC): Hello, am I talking to Mr. XYZ?

Restaurant Manager (RM): Hello, yes you are. Who are you?

RC: Hello, my name is ABC and I am calling you on behalf of Company 123 as we would like to know more about Mr. Mustafa Toga?

RM: Which Mustafa Toga?

RC: Well, Mr. Toga applied for a position at the Company 123 and gave you as a reference. Are you sure you do not know him?

RM: Yes, I am sure. I do not know him. (Meanwhile, my ex-manager was thinking that there might be some new kitchen staff members who he had not had the chance to meet).

RC: Well, that is strange. Mr. Mustafa Toga gave your contact details and so I am surprised that you do not know him.

RM: (My ex-manager was doing all he could to think. At last, the penny dropped) Ah, you mean Musti. Of course, I know Musti. Mustafa….

When my ex-manager told me this, I was slightly astonished; however, in the end we laughed a lot and he told me that he gave very positive feedback. I really do not know what would have actually happened if he had not remembered me. It just highlights that even the most obvious things can change the outcome.

Look out for Other Options

Aside from writing down your experiences, connecting via LinkedIn to the interviewer, writing a follow-up email to the hiring manager, and notifying your references, there is not much you can do until the deadline approaches and hopefully the phone rings delivering the positive news. Or perhaps this is what you think. If you really want something you need to make an effort to achieve it.

While the corporate culture and the work environment can vary from company to company, certain roles, departments, and positions are similar in all larger organisation. If you really do want the position you applied for, I wish you all the best for obtaining it. If you do not get this job at this particular company, it is not the end of the world. You are young and have a long career in front of you. What is important for you is to simply start your career and find your way.

You should review what you wrote down regarding the point, "why are you excited to join this company?" Is it because you liked the career path you can develop? Or is it the team you met and will likely work with? Is it the product or service the company offers? Or is it the hiring manager because he was very promising and seemed to be a great leader to work for? Is it the office because it is very fancy and cool…?

With this information, you can narrow down your search when looking for other options. If you liked the type of industry the company is working in, then you should look for comparable companies. As an example, if you had your original interview at KPMG for a "Financial Advisory" role and you really liked the job description, interview and the vision and mission, then you are likely to find similar/same roles at other large accounting firms such PricewaterhouseCoopers (PwC), Deloitte, and Ernst & Young.

Check if those companies have openings in your city or somewhere you could imagine living, and you can also check some smaller firms to start with. Big names do not always mean the best place to work, and smaller companies often have a more family-type atmosphere where the work climate is very supportive. As you are a newbie and have not had much work experience, you might consider going to a smaller firm to learn the basics.

Imagine, while you wait for the response from KMPG you are invited for a job interview at, say, Deloitte. If they ask you and you let them know that you are actively looking for a position as a financial advisor and are actually also currently talking to KPMG, the interest in you will increase. That said, you will still need to do all the relevant things and preparation you have done for the other interview. And if you still do not get an answer from KPMG after a week or ten days or the deadline they gave you, it is now time to call them up and kindly ask what the situation is. If they cannot provide a clear answer or postpone the deadline for the final decision, just make them aware that you are also talking to Deloitte and are quite advanced in the hiring process. This move is likely to create an urgency and increase the interest in your candidature.

Receiving the Contract

After the long-awaited phone call or email, you finally receive the positive notification that you are accepted to your dream job. Congratulation! You made it.

Naturally, you are thrilled and cannot wait to sign the job agreement. While it is absolutely understandable that you jump around and celebrate, you need to ensure to sleep one day or two over it before you sign it. Before signing it, find a calm moment to carefully read the contract. An employment contract means a commitment, and accordingly, it is a serious life decision since you will hopefully be carrying out the role for several months or years.

You need to check that all the points you agreed on are listed and if some are missing get a clear understanding of why they are not on the contract. You might also encounter unfamiliar words in the agreement, which you should list and double check with the HR department or hiring manager in order you fully understand them. Here comes a list of the points to clarify when you start the contract review step:

Starting Date and Working Hours

Remember that when starting a job, you will likely work 35–40 hours a week and probably have 20–30 vacation days per year. In other words, your free time will be very limited and valuable. If there is any long-planned desired trips or any private situations that mean you may want to consider pushing back the start date – now is the time. During the job interview, you will normally be asked when the ideal start date is for you. Think about the above and choose the start date wisely. The companies will make a big effort to get you to start immediately. On the one hand they would like a strong candidate to make an impact on the business, and on the other hand, they want to secure the deal to avoid the candidates going to another company. Therefore, companies are eager to put the start date as the earliest possible. If you have a plausible reason and explain it to the hiring manager, I am sure you will find a compromise on the start date.

Job Title and Description

Of course, what you read on the job description and what you talked about during the interview with your new employer should match with the description on the job agreement. You want to think twice and clear up any mismatch regarding responsibilities and also title before signing.

Salary and Bonuses

This is most likely to be the first figure you will try to find in the contract. Not only you should ensure that the figure is the same as you negotiated or were offered, but it is also important that you understand how and when you will be paid. Understand which parts your compensation includes. Do you only have a fixed (a.k.a. base) part? Is your salary divided into commission or bonuses or other benefits granted by your employer? You should also get a sense of how much money you will earn per month on a net basis. Meaning, understand what the tax and social welfare contributions will be that you will need to deduct from your monthly salary, which will in turn then give you the net income. You need to also understand how often you get paid. For instance, in Spain companies often divide the annual base salary by 14 and you receive the representing amount each month. Additionally, in June (Summer) and December (Christmas) you then receive the 13th and 14th salary in addition. You need to do some maths or ask the hiring manager for guidance in order to understand what you will earn as a secured base salary. This will also help you to better plan your life. A basic example: can I afford a private apartment, or should I share a flat? On top of this, check if all the other benefits that were promised during the interview are also listed, such as health insurance, company car, company mobile phone, restaurant vouchers, or others.

Holidays and Sick Leave

Make sure you understand the rules and laws of the country that you will be working in before reviewing this section. While from country to country the law varies, it is hard to compare your home country's regulation if you are about to start your career abroad with the destination country. Therefore, get an understanding or help if something is unclear.

Termination Terms and Conditions

You should understand what type of behaviours might lead to an immediate termination of your job, in order to avoid those mistakes. Furthermore, certain contracts have the condition of a probation time. This is a trial period where the employer can lay off employees without any reason or penalties. It can vary from three to six months, and in some cases up to one year. After that period, it is common that your contract will automatically change to an indefinite one. There is also something called notice period. This is generally also listed in the contract. The notice period provides the time for how long needs to be respected if one of the parties decides to terminate the contract. This duration can be anywhere between two weeks and several months. For instance, if you want to leave the company due to whatever circumstances, you will need to calculate the notice period before you jump to the next opportunity. This time should help both parties to better prepare for the next step. In this situation, it will allow some time for your current employer to look for an adequate replacement for you without worrying that the work you were doing stays still.

Signs You Should Turn down a Job Offer

You were very keen and put a lot of effort into the job process, and so not accepting a job offer can be a very difficult decision to make. However, you are going to spend many months and years at this company, and hopefully it fits what you expect and desire. The salary, especially, should not be your first decision-making criteria. Let's imagine you have two offers from different companies in hand:

Company A: offer looks very attractive and the salary is 20% more than Company B offers. You also have a very important sounding job title. On the other hand, during the job interview you had the chance to meet some of your potential new colleagues but could not really sense their motivation and enthusiasm in working there. Lastly, you did not really like your future manager and witnessed the managing style they had and could not identify with it.

Company B: salary is decent but less than the offer of Company A. On top of this, your title does not really sound fancy nor cool. However, from the first moment that you talked with the recruiter and entered the office you liked it. The working environment was very encouraging, and the people seemed to be very motivated. The team was also quite diverse. In addition, you had a very positive feeling about the hiring manager and felt that you could learn a lot from them. The career path they described also matches your plan.

Tough call? It probably is. But think about where you currently are, entry level. You still have a long way to go. During the early years of your career especially, you should bet your commitment on a company that really offers a good training and development plan. You should be like a sponge, striving to absorb as much knowledge and new skills as possible.

The good thing with money is that it also has eyes and will find you. Did I say eyes? And did you think "hold on, what do you mean by that?" Let me explain. As you learn and master your role, you must gain new skills to optimise it, have passion and enthusiasm in what you are doing, and in turn you will be noticed. With that mindset, you will make early wins and impact, and upper management will hear and know about you. You establish your brand. In the long term, you will be recognised as a great asset and people who have more compelling roles will reach out to you.

In the short term, if you continue being humble and establish a good professional relationship with your manager, they will enjoy having you on the team and help you to grow. Of course, here and there you will need to agree on milestones with your manager and understand how to get to the next level. If you achieve and outperform those goals, your promotion should be on the horizon. If money is your only motivator, you might consider Company A. If not, my recommendation would be that you listen to your gut and start your career where you have excellent learning opportunities.

Chapter 4

—

On Job

The First 30-60-90 Days at Your New Job

Now that you have made it through the interview process and landed your dream job, what is next? The real work starts now, and not just the work itself, but also the work on your branding and development.

I want to emphasise again the power of the first impression. Your willingness to learn and eagerness to create value and be a great team player will be determined during the first weeks and month, as will what your manager and colleagues think about you.

Very often, companies have a 30-60-90 days onboarding programme with certain goals and milestones. If your company has such a plan it is great. If not, do not worry and proactively build one. Your manager can help you to prioritise what is important and what is not. I would also urge you to have at least a weekly meeting (ideally on a Friday or Monday) to review your progress with your manager, put goals for the upcoming week and most importantly get feedback. This way you naturally establish a relationship with your manager and also get to know each other better. Understand your manager's style and ensure you know what is important for them and adapt yourself accordingly. If your manager sets goals for you, ensure you really understand what they are looking for as an outcome and by when they are expecting it. Do your best to respect the deadline and if there is something blocking you from finishing the task, let your manager know in a timely manner and ask for a suggestion. Ideally, you have already put some thought into it and so can present these thoughts to them about how to overcome the challenge.

One of the first goals will be that you get up to speed, and the above-described plan will give you the structure to get there. However, it is also key that you set yourself a goal or milestones. From time to time, I ask new hires at our welcome meeting during the first week to take a piece of paper and write down what they would love to learn and achieve after six months. I let them sign it and stick it to my wall. Obviously, there is no penalty if they do not achieve it, but I think it is important that you always have personal development goals linked to your career.

During the first weeks, companies tend to overload the new hires with tons of information. Web-based training, instructor-led sessions, product demonstrations, certain software solutions they use, internal policies and processes, and similar. It is very tempting to be scared, frustrated and doubt your abilities to master everything. The golden rule is not to lose sight of the light at the end of the tunnel; stay positive, keep calm, talk to your manager and talk to your colleagues. Nobody expects you know everything by heart after the first 90 days. Even if it is written on the plan, you have to learn to walk before you run.

When I first started my professional career, I remember that I sometimes had no clue about what was going on. As I mentioned earlier, I had worked many years in the gastronomy business as a waiter but never had any experience of a professional office job. There were a lot of new words and certain new processes that I was not familiar with, which made me feel very insecure. I was not even used to sitting eight hours a day, forty hours a week, on a chair at my desk in front of the laptop. It took me some time to adapt to it. Fortunately, mother nature was good to me and I am actually a very optimistic and positive person and love to smile. With that, I quickly established a relationship with many colleagues and was talking with them and asking for their support. As most of them also went through this period, they were happily sharing their experiences and letting me know what actually really matters, which helped me to overcome the insecurity.

You will likely also be assigned to a mentor. The mentor is there to help and guide you throughout your onboarding. You should also adapt yourself to your mentor. Naturally, you will have many questions. Understand the best way to address them and set an operating rhythm. It could be that you meet daily, just quickly for 15 minutes to go through your questions, or perhaps your mentor will prefer you to ask questions as they pop up. Listen carefully to what your mentor says and note it down if needed and avoid asking the same question over and over. Keep in mind that your mentor has a regular job and now has less time to accomplish it as they are also investing time in you.

One suggestion that I commonly pose to our new hires is that they, of course, should use the mentor if they have a question, but should also check with other team members. This in turn allows you not to bombard your mentor with questions and more importantly helps you to establish a relationship with other team members.

If you are lucky there is another new hire or someone who recently started. If there is a new hire you may want to consider doing some of the web-based training together, if feasible. These pieces of training can be very long and actually quite boring. There is a German saying that means something along the lines of "suffering shared is half as painful". Moreover, it is far more fun if you have an interactive session rather than doing it alone. Somehow, going through this journey together tends to bond new hires.

Ten years ago, when I started my professional career, we had three weeks of intense development sessions with all the new hires at that time. We were a group of 40-50 people. At the end of these three weeks, I made a lot of great new colleagues and friends. I still have regular contact with two of them. After a while, we all went down different paths, however, through this connection we helped each other a lot and optimised our connections if someone was looking for a new job opportunity or needed something.

Bear in mind that it is likely that you will never again have that much time dedicated to learning and your development. Slowly but surely, after a couple of weeks, the business and workload will also reach you. This is actually a good thing because I strongly believe that learning by doing is much more effective in this sense. The point I am making is to use the time wisely at the beginning to learn, as very soon you will not have much time due to the business duties.

Your New Colleagues

While your first goal is a no-brainer, to get up to speed, there are other things you need to do simultaneously at the beginning. Establishing a relationship with your new team members is one of those things. Generally, at the beginning your manager will be sending an email to the team to introduce you, and typically some of the co-workers will answer with "welcome" and "let me know if you have any questions". This is a great invitation and you should capitalise on it. People like to give advice and if you ask them for it you demonstrate subconsciously that you respect them and value their opinion. That will help you to stand out and make you a likable person. In addition, go with your peers for lunch breaks and observe them. There is a certain group dynamic in each team that can also give you clues about who's who in the zoo. Understanding the personality types of your peers will really help you to climb the career ladder. Who is nice and supportive? Who has a lot of knowledge? Who is positive? Who is negative? Who has their own agenda? Who actually does not want to be at the company?

Let's face it. There are those type of friends who you have known since your childhood and sandbox time, who you know inside and out and can trust blindly. And there are those friends you make later during university or at work. Don't get me wrong, I am not suggesting that you cannot trust or make any newer great friendships with colleagues or as a young adult. However, as a kid your only goal was to play and have fun. As an adult, people experience life transitions such as entering the workforce or establishing a family. With that, people have their own agenda and way of looking at things.

It is crucial for you to observe and analyse which of your colleagues are actually lifting you up and who are actually complaining at almost every possible moment and dragging you down. Spend more time with co-workers who lift you up. Not only will it make you happier, but it will also energise you and in stressful times can help to keep you calm.

Your Ecosystem

Another suggestion I often make is that the key to your success is to build your ecosystem. The ecosystem means the people from various departments working in your organisation. The better you understand how your organisation works as a whole and which key departments work closely with your department and have an impact on your work, the better you are prepared to be successful.

Let's look at an example: you work in the sales department and cover the Italian market, in charge of selling a certain product called ABC. You should understand who else is interested and is measured on the successful selling of this product and may even also have an objective against it. If you identify certain other colleagues, you may want to work jointly on a business plan on how to best cover the market and split the work.

Furthermore, find out which other departments can help you. The sales department is working hand in hand with the marketing department, and so find out who is in charge of promoting the product ABC in Italy. Establish a relationship with them and understand what type of campaigns or marketing activities this person is doing and how you can help each other. Understand where the outcome (normally called leads) of those activities go, meaning if the marketing department sends to a bunch of customers or new prospects an email about ABC, you want to know the list of the target audience and who actually responded and showed interest. If you follow up on those leads you are more likely to sell your product.

To continue on this example, there are many more departments who can support you. The pre-sales department with technical gurus who know the features of the product inside out can help you to run product demos and to show the customer the value of ABC. Be genuinely interested to understand your organisation, and with that, you will find key departments and people who can help you to be successful. It is important that you do not take things for granted. Just because you are selling ABC, the marketing department is not obliged to create hundreds of leads for you.

It is very helpful to build a mindset of a win-win situation and make it into a routine whereby you first listen to understand your opponents and then work on being understood. Stephen Covey, an American author and businessman described this principle in his famous book, which also has the same title, "The 7 Habits of Highly Effective People".

I can only recommend that you buy this book as it will give a tremendous amount of advice and new perspectives in order to look at things and be more successful. People often think that in order for someone to win, someone else has to lose. But it is not always like this in sport, for example. Understand what is important for the other person and how this person's work is measured. Based on that, find options for where you can synergise your efforts and be both more successful together.

Coming back to our example between you as the salesperson and the marketing department, make an effort to clearly understand what your marketing co-worker's goal is and how you can work jointly to create a win-win situation. If the goal of your marketing person is to run one webcast with at least 20 attendees, help them to promote this event and get as many people registered to it as possible. You may also suggest that the webcast should also highlight and cover your product ABC's benefits. With that, the attendees also become very relevant for you to follow up to see if they have a need.

If everyone works individually there might be a missed opportunity. You have most likely heard the expression "the whole is greater than the sum of its parts". This is also called synergy. And it is one of the seven habits, among the above described "Think Win-

Win" and "Seek first to understand, then to be understood" that Stephen Covey describes in his book.

Confident but Humble

When we are humble, we are demonstrating that we are not perfect and need help and cannot do everything straight from the beginning alone or correctly. You do not want to come across as an arrogant person that knows everything. Be open-minded and ask for support if needed. Appreciate the people who are helping you and do not take credit for work that you did not do yourself. Highlight the person(s) who helped you to accomplish certain tasks and wins.

At the same time, you need to work on making an impact and focus on early wins. Try to understand what the team's priority and current challenges are and think about how you can bring your expertise into the game. Think big and try things out. As a new hire, for a certain time you have the luxury of being able to make mistakes. Nobody would blame a new hire for a mistake. Of course, this is depending on the level of the mistakes – there are certainly limits that everyone, no matter how long they are with the company, needs to respect. I can only appeal to your common sense here.

You can already make an impact with the little things. Just because there are habits for doing things in a certain way, it does not mean there is no room for your creativity. As an example, in business meetings, we use PowerPoint to share slides and highlight information. These meetings can be long, and it is hard to keep the attention of the audience. While PowerPoint itself allows for a lot of room for creativity, with cool features to bring across your message, most people only have a basic knowledge and usage of the tool. With your fresh energy, you may think about investing some time in learning more about PowerPoint and stand out during meetings when you present.

Or better still, go even further. Challenge the status quo. A couple of years ago we gave some interns a task to present a topic. Those interns used a different presentation software instead of PowerPoint. They used Prezi. Not only due to the content but also the way in which they told their story and made it more visual through the use of the tool really blew the minds of the audience. Including mine. I was so impressed, and it was such a nice and fresh look at things rather than using the traditional solutions. For some further meetings, I used Prezi myself. It is never too late to learn new things!

Now I don't want you to go out there and question mark every single software or process your employer is using. I just want to encourage you not to be shy in bringing up an idea if you think you can improve or do certain things more effectively or efficiently. If they like your idea that's great, but if not, do not take it personally. At least you are showing some proactiveness.

Another way of making a quick win is to understand and discover more about what your manager appreciates. Arrange your tasks accordingly to support your manager's and team's goals as well.

After working for almost 1.5 years at my first employer, I decided to move from Ireland to Spain and work for another IT company and continue in the sales department. Two weeks into the new job, we had a previously planned meeting. At this meeting, organised by my manager, we had important Sales VP managers, field sales representatives with a lot of sales experience, our team and the sales enablement team present. During the meeting, we had some product training with a follow-up role play session. Some senior managers were playing the role of a customer and our sales representatives needed to try to position our solution. Weeks before, the sales team members were already being provided with a case study with a little more background information to be better prepared for the role plays.

I could see that many of my new colleagues were nervous, probably mainly as some senior managers were present. As I was the new kid on the block, I was safe because nobody would dare to pick a newcomer. Before the next break, we had two role plays. After observing those and with the skills I had learned from my previous employer I was very confident that I could do it as well. During the break, I went to my manager and I told him that so far, I thought it was very interesting and that I would like to try it as well. He was very surprised and asked me if I had read the case study, which I denied. He was even more surprised, but with a smile he said, "why not". He then told one of the senior sales managers who then approached me. The senior sales manager scanned me and then looked directly at me. His eyes were saying "are you sure, kid?" He then told me that I did not need to do it, but I kindly responded with a smile that I would like to try it.

After the break, they announced that I would be the next one. Most of my colleagues were wondering what was going on and thought it was unfair. However, I went up and did exactly what I described earlier during the section discussing sales. I tried to personally connect and bond with my potential client and asked some relevant questions to understand their current situation and identify certain business needs. After twenty minutes of role play, without mentioning anything about our product (which I barely knew about anyway), I agreed on a next step with the customer to further discuss and show how we might support them. Not only did I gain the respect of my colleagues, but it left a big impression in the minds of many of the attendees, including the senior leaders. Nine years later, one of the attendees still refers to that session about my performance.

My point is not to demonstrate to you how great I performed on that occasion. What I am trying to do is to make you understand that you need to try things out. Have the courage and gut to take a risk. Of course, I could have been grilled during the role play and embarrassed myself. But I went up there because I calculated the risk and knew what I could do. Worse case, the newcomer label would have saved me.

Therefore, I want to encourage you to try things out, and then try and try again. Do not be scared, take risks and get out of the comfort zone.

I recently saw the following post on LinkedIn, which I liked a lot and re-shared:

> "I've missed more than 9,000 shots in my career. I've lost almost 300 games. 26 times I've been trusted to take the game's winning shot and missed. I've failed over and over and over again in my life and that's why I succeed."

This is a quote from Michael Jordan, one of the greatest basketball players of all time. Take a risk as it is associated with fun. Make mistakes and quickly stand up again. Each failure also brings a learning opportunity on how to do it better. Believe in yourself and your capabilities and skill set. Do not centre your thoughts on the mistakes. Instead, focus on what you have already accomplished and where your eagerness and dedication will take you next.

Demonstrate Your Hunger for Knowledge

Depending on the complexity of the work and the structure of your onboarding plan, you will probably need around six weeks to obtain a basic understanding of how things work. Again, this can vary from company to company. It does not mean that you will know everything after this period, but it is important that you have your mindset programmed on constant learning and trying. You are too damn young and early in your career to get comfortable, be in your own bubble and only do what needs to be done.

An ex-colleague of mine was this type of worker. At that time, our office layout was with cubicle desks, and each desk was divided by a wall, so you could not see your colleagues unless you stood up and went to their space. Despite this, this ex-colleague did everything in his power not to be visible, and there were rumours that he had a tunnel under his desk that he was using every morning to sneak out from the office. He was very quiet, almost invisible, but was performing decently as far as we could see when our manager shared team results and individual contributions to the overall achievement. I have nothing against solid contributors who may not be as visible as others. However, I doubt this is a good strategy to learn and climb the career ladder.

Be out there, be visible, go the extra mile, look for opportunities and voluntarily sign up for tasks and projects if they come along. Even if you are not 100% sure how to correctly finish the task or what its gain to you might be, if you are offered an exciting opportunity, jump on it and say "yes".

Naturally, you will first become comfortable with your office desk neighbours. Once you know them, go around and meet other people. Learn from them how they are doing things. By now, you know that people like to talk about themselves and are willing to share knowledge. As you are a new starter, psychologically, you would not be considered as a threat to them, and they would not have an interest conflict sharing their knowledge. Ideally, you give them something back in return. Maybe they have some projects going on that you can support, and by doing so learn.

Meeting other colleagues and getting out of your comfort zone should be one of the habits you establish for yourself, as discussed when focusing on extending your ecosystem. Nobody is expecting that you are Mother Teresa and that you devote all your resources in helping others at your company. Just be smart about it. Understand carefully what your manager expects and what deliveries you have in order to respect a certain deadline. That should be your first priority. If you then find the time, which you should, do the above-described activities. If it means you need to do some extra hours in your early career, then do it. This investment will pay off.

10 Things You Should Avoid at Work

There are some unwritten rules at work and in a professional environment. Some might be tolerated, some might be custom of few employees, and some can turn to big mistakes and lead to the termination of your contract.

1. Disregard Office Hours

Let's start with getting to work. You may need to commute in the early rush hour to work. Of course, certain things like traffic jams, crowds, and trains are not your fault. However, if it is resulting in you being late to work it will have an impact on your brand. Let's imagine that the normal office hours are between 9 am and 6 pm. Around 15 minutes after the official starting hour, 95% of the employees will be at their place (unless there is a meeting, or they are off). If you are arriving late two or three times a month, this will be noticed. The upside of this is that you can control it. How? Leave home twenty minutes earlier in order to arrive before 9 am. Would you like to be remembered as the one who is one of the first in the office or the one who is usually late?

Further advice relates to the time you are leaving. Some folks and interns I observe cannot wait for 6 pm. At exactly 6 pm they gather their things and are out. It seems that they are bored and cannot wait to leave the office. Have you ever wondered why time seems to move faster when you're having fun? Simply because if you are having fun you do not look at the time and your attention is on other things. The same goes at work when you are focusing on a certain activity or task. Time will fly, and you will enjoy what you do. When it is 6 pm, let the crowd leave the office. Spend a few more minutes noting down certain key learnings of your day. Check your Outlook Calendar to see what tomorrow looks like. Are there important meetings that you should be prepared for? Is there anyone important coming that means you should dress up? Is there any meeting at 9 am sharp that means you do not want to be arriving late? This activity won't take you more than ten minutes. By 6.10 pm you will probably be with a few others who will be remembered as always staying longer in the office. That will have a positive mark on how your manager perceives you.

2. Dress Too Casually

If we dress up for important meetings and occasions that means something, right? With the dress, we influence how people see us. This still goes for your normal work, even once you are hired and working for the company you want to work. Respect the dress code of your company or your department. If "smart casual" is the dress code, then the weighting should be on "smart" and not "casual". Ripped jeans, t-shirts with prints and your Sunday jumper are not smart casual. See it from this perspective: dressing well will boost your confidence and you never know to whom you are going to run into in the office kitchen or elevator. It is better to wear something very neat and appropriate.

3. Drink Alcohol

Gone are the days when you could go to university after a great night out, still with alcohol surging through your blood, or to continue sleeping to recover from the hangover and dismiss the first class or the entire day. Would you like it if the pilot of the next plane you will catch has alcohol in his blood from the night before? Can you imagine if Ronaldo or Messi were to play drunk football? You couldn't, right? The same applies to the expectations of your employer. You really do not want to be caught being drunk or smelling of alcohol. Occasionally you may have team nights out, events or happy hours at the office where alcohol is offered. Drinking one or two beers with your colleagues is totally OK, but not knowing your limits and what you can tolerate is NOT OK. It is pointless to list all the potential mistakes you might make if you are drunk, which can have serious consequences on your career.

4. Waste Your Working Hours on Private Matters

Nowadays it is not totally out of the ordinary to check your social media from time to time or make an important private phone call. That said, be careful with how much time you are spending and what exactly you are doing. For instance, there are people who are caught downloading movies at work. Others have private phone calls on an important and serious topic in the open office space where everyone can hear. Some listen to music and do not even realise that people around them can also hear it. Few have a side job or project and use the work hours of their real job to do them. You are getting paid to get your real job done. While some things might be tolerated, you do not want to overstretch the limit.

5. Express Opinions on Religion, Race, Gender, Sexual Orientation, and Political Views

Diversity can be a great asset for you to utilise and learn from. Companies who invest in a diverse workforce obtain better outcomes and have new ideas when brainstorming or are trying to solve a problem. You should feel privileged if you work in a diverse team. While it is OK to talk about what you did last weekend or talk about the newest movie or the last great match or concert, it is NOT OK to make your personal belief and opinion vocal if it is crossing your colleagues' freedom. The workplace is not the right field to talk about politics. If you have an opinion on a certain sensitive non-work-related topic or person, keep it to yourself. Watch out that you are not dragged into a conversation that can be discriminating and/or make your colleagues feel uncomfortable or even harassed.

6. Disrespect Co-Workers and Customers

People are often stressed at work. There are deadlines to respect or goals to achieve and many things are not working as planned. Welcome to reality. While stress is OK and can be something positive, you need to control that stress and ensure it does not turn into anger. If you are angry you are likely do things that you will regret when it is too late. Screaming around, yelling at someone or responding with a very angry email will negatively influence your reputation. Or worse, can cost you your job. You need to learn to be patient and stay calm. Do not immediately reply. If it is possible to take a little break, have a walk outside in the fresh air, or even better, sleep one night over it if it is feasible. That will help you to regain your calm and allow you to form a rational rather than emotional response.

7. Burn Bridges

As with the previous point, throughout your career you will encounter times where you may dislike or feel unable to make any sort of connection with some of your colleagues. While this is part of life, ensure you remain professional. You do not want to talk badly or gossip or start a "war" with this person. You never know how things shape up and maybe one day this person is promoted and becomes your manager. Therefore, your goal should be to build, instead of burn bridges.

8. Reject Certain Tasks and Duties

We talked earlier about the fact that the dynamics of business and companies need to constantly change. If there is an urgency and a project that needs to be done it could be that your team needs to step up and accomplish it. Just because a certain task was not listed in your job description does not mean that you should refuse to do the job. You really do not want to be the person who often says, "this is not my job". If certain things need to be done, they need to be done. Your manager and your company are looking for people who get things done.

9. Disclose Too Much Private Information

Unfortunately, like everywhere, gossip does not stop at the office entrance. Not only should you stay away from gossip and people who tend mainly to gossip, but you should also ensure that you do not feed it. What I mean by that is that you should control how much private information about yourself you want to reveal at work. Your private life, your sex life, your crazy weekend out, your personal issues with your partner or family are your private things. I would suggest you place limits on unpacking your whole self at work.

10. Be Impatient

In my opinion, one of the biggest virtues to have is patience. Not only in your private life but also at work especially, as business is not always smooth and certain processes do not always run perfectly. There will be many curves, adjustments, and tweaks in the way business is done and if you do not accept changes or do not allow time to digest and adapt to them you will become impatient. Impatience is like an invisible thing in you, taking control of you and resulting in you doing or saying things that you will likely regret. Conversely, being patient allows us to master difficult situations easier and helps us to keep the right perspective. Furthermore, it keeps us away from being frustrated and angry.

In today's world, you can instantly obtain almost everything that you want. You are lost, you ask Google maps. You want the newest sneaker, Amazon brings it to you in 24 hours. You want to watch a movie, Netflix offers you hundreds of movies to choose from. You are hungry, Deliveroo promises to get you your order in an average of 32 minutes. If this is the standard you are used too that might be a blessing; however, at the same time it may be a misfortune. In (business) life, hard work does not always pay off immediately. It takes time. You may have certain expectations to see prompt results, and of course with that, more success and ultimately your next promotion. Rather than focusing on time and quick results, it is better to focus on actions we can control. Focus on producing the good outcome your company wants helps you to further grow and master your role. In the end, hard work will always pay off.

Is This Your Dream Job?

Assuming that after a year or so on the job, when the dust has settled, you have obtained a better understanding of the role, the purpose, the organisation and you have gained solid knowledge in being successful in that role, you may then want to ask, "does this role fulfil me?"

To begin with, I want to clarify that you should be realistic when answering this question for yourself. If you did not make it to a manager or a senior role, that is absolutely normal. If you did not make a huge impact and save the world, that is also probably the norm. The key elements you should question are:

- Am I (still) constantly learning and growing in this role?
- Do you I have the drive to go to work every morning?
- Do I love what I do?

In particular, the first two questions are highly important in your early career life. When your learning curve is stagnating, and each morning you have inner fights and look for reasons not to go to work, you should seriously consider if the role you are doing is really what you want to do. It seems like a no-brainer, right? But do you know how many people I have met pursuing a role that they eventually do not like and constantly complain about it? The sad part is that these people do not want to take control of their happiness. Instead of having the guts and deciding to change, they chose the easy road – continuing to do what they were doing. Some due to the money they earn, others because they are afraid to make a change, and few accept this as a fact.

You should have joy at work. It should give you a purpose outside of the monetary gain. It should make you happy and you should love it. Watch out, there is a fine line between expecting it from the job and looking to find it at the job. And before you make any decision you should proactively work on finding it yourself. Many companies have clear expectation on the outcome of the work, but at the same time empower their employees to achieve it in their own way.

You may know the expression "all roads lead to Rome". In other words, if your company expects you to be in Rome (the outcome) you may have a lot of room for creativity and find your "way" to get there. By doing so you learn new things and will likely find your joy as you can do the things you like. Before making a decision regarding the role as such, you may want to also distinguish the company and certain processes. If you really like the company but not the role, understand what tasks you do not like. If you, for example, work in sales and really do not like to call customers, that's OK. List the things you do not like and when you search for another role keep that list in your hand. Why? Well, I have met many people working in sales who do not like it and who finally made the decision to leave and look for another opportunity. The funny part was that they were starting in another company as a salesperson! Just because you change the colour of the company logo, it does not mean the role itself will change.

This also applies to processes. If you are working for a big company and the processes are slow, which makes you angry and want to quit, just think twice about it. Just because the grass looks greener on the other side does not mean that the other side has it better. Unfortunately, bigger organisations can be complex, and processes can take time and are sometimes very unclear. If this is the only reason why you would think to change the company, I would suggest that you look to control your behaviour and how you react to these circumstances. If you are still unsatisfied you may want to change to a company that is much smaller where the processes are faster.

Overall, focus instead on the things you do not like and identify what you love and what your passion is. As opposed to looking for the perfect job in the description, look out for the role and company that best suits your passion and allows you the freedom to explore and execute them.

Coming back to the example of liking the company but not the role, what you should do is to reach out to your ecosystem. Understand what exactly they do and evaluate which roles are existing at your company and how they may be a good fit for you. Meanwhile, stay positive and ensure you continue executing your current role in an excellent manner. In addition, have an open discussion with your manager and share your thoughts and work on achieving your milestones. Even though you want to leave your manager's team, your manager should be interested in supporting your move into another team. This is called internal mobility and even your manager will benefit out of your move as it will motivate other team members and demonstrate that if you do a good job the company will support an internal move. If you make the decision to change, do not become desperate and jump on the next coming opportunity. The chances of you being unsatisfied again soon are very high.

Now, as you have working experience and a better understanding of the hiring process, use this to your advantage. Qualify and gain a very good understanding of what the new role and the company is about and double check that they fit well into your list of what you like and what you don't.

Chapter 5

—

Work-Life Balance

Work, Life & the Balance Between the Two

I am genuinely interested in observing people. This could be a result of the combination of the various things that I have done so far in my life: the many years I worked as a waiter and now as a director, the many times I travelled and met new people, and probably my being me. Throughout these observations, as well as reading about the topic of happiness and being successful, I have made a list of patterns that I personally think play a key role in your happiness and at the same time being successful.

A Simple Recipe for Being Happy and Successful

Here are, in my opinion, the main ingredients for a more productive, energetic and motivated life:

Goals and Rewarding Yourself

Think big and dream high. After that exercise, ask yourself "what do I need to do to get there?" Always have goals in life. If you want to be happy in life, you need progress in life. If you stagnate you will feel bored and start questioning yourself and your life. To avoid this, work with goals. Have constant goals in life. It does not need to be something big every time, such as running a marathon. Start small and work step by step to reach your dream. Once you reach your target, treat yourself well. There is no harm in rewarding yourself. This tactic particularly helped me when I was a student. I needed to work part-time simultaneously with my studies and in order not to lose the momentum, I was undertaking a minimum number of exams each semester that I needed to as a goal. And when I reached that target, I treated myself with a nice trip. A perfect win-win situation!

Practice a Sport

People spend hours in front of the TV or laptop screen and argue that they do not have time for doing sport. I am not sure if it is still a secret, but I can guarantee you that sports can be an essential element of being happy. It positively influences so many areas of life. This includes the physical benefits where endorphins can impact your mood and help you to work out the stress of your body. It will also help you to be in shape and boost your self-confidence. And, it transmits so many crucial values that are important in life and the workplace: willpower, team spirit, discipline, winning mentality and stretching the limits. There are plenty of types of sport, so choose the one you like. Three to four times a week, each time around an hour should be manageable to fit into your busy calendar. It is important that you practice a sport that you like and find joy in. If you dislike swimming there is no point investing your time in practicing that. Is Zumba yours? Or HIIT? Or hiking? The good thing is that you can decide.

Morning Routine

Do you know why Mark Zuckerberg wears the same thing every day? Steve Jobs also wore the same outfit every day. And many others do it too. The main reason is that those people want to avoid mental fatigue. Mental what? Mental fatigue. Fatigue means extreme tiredness resulting from mental or physical effort. Human beings only have a limited volume of energy and willpower each day. With each decision we make, it gets drained away. And guess what, we make hundreds if not thousands of conscious and unconscious decisions and thoughts every single day. Put it this way: every single decision, even if it is small or unimportant, will make your brain tired and throughout the day have an impact on the remaining decisions you will make.

Therefore, many successful people have a morning routine to limit spending decision power on less relevant topics. A morning routine will also help you to start the day more smoothly with some calm moments before the rush of the city and business life. This moment can help you to sort your mind and ideally get you to think about the things you want to accomplish that day. You will probably dislike what I am about to write now, but you should also consider waking up earlier. Why? Plenty of CEOs and successful people swear on the benefits of waking up early. If this is not enough, just think about why we have traffic jams in rush hours? Or think about how crowded the fitness centre is around 6–8pm when people go after work. Or restaurants and other common things people do. Did you ever do grocery shopping on Saturday morning? Next time go on Saturday at a time where people usually have lunch or dinner. You will see how much more pleasant it is. If you wake up early, you not only have many more calm moments in the morning, but you also save more time and can shift certain activities from peak time to a less crowded time. Waking up early does not mean you should be restless. It is still very important that you get your seven to eight hours sleep each night, meaning you will go to bed earlier. The good thing is that you will be so exhausted that you won't have any problems falling asleep.

Read

They say reading is like feeding your brain. I must admit I did not like to read when I was young, and if there was one thing that I disliked more than reading, it was the topic of psychology. I did not believe in it nor could I understand people studying it. Ironically, due to my role, psychology became very relevant and, in the end, I really loved to study and read more about this subject. It really helped me personally to grow and be more successful. Of course, this depends on what type of book you read. However, the books that I was reading had a lot of practical tips that you could try out and explore how they work. Through that, you get a feeling for what works for you and you can make those things into a habit. Find a topic or subject you like and start to read about it.

Try New Things

Same old, same old? Or do you spice up your life and routines with new things? Phineas Taylor Barnum, an American showman, politician, and businessman once said, "comfort is the enemy of progress".

Of course, it is easier to always go to the same few restaurants we always go, and of course, it is easier to do the known things and follow our programmed habits. However, if you want to personally grow and be proud of yourself you need to progress and try new things out. The positive side of it is that you can choose whatever you want to try out and learn as a new skill or hobby. It is no longer like it was in school or university where the learning plan was already pre-scheduled. Try new things out, widen your knowledge and meet new people. It does not need to be something complex, and it is never too late for anything. As an example: I started to learn jump rope when I was 37 years old! I liked it so much that it is now a part of my work out sessions.

Surround Yourself with Positive People

Do you agree with the saying "show me who your friends are, and I'll tell you who you are"? The people you spend time with are shaping your personality, the way you see the world, the way you judge what is good, what is normal and what is possible. Some people make it a habit to see the negative in everything, always blame others and are afraid to move out of their comfort zone. Rumours are their oxygen, and being a pessimist, their engine. Negative people barely picture a happy outcome or great result, and they often imagine that most things will go wrong. Whilst positive people will lift you up, negative people will do the opposite. Choose wisely with whom you spend your time. Positive people and friends will help to bring out the best in you.

Life is full of ups and downs, and positive friends are there to celebrate your ups with you and guide you through tough times, helping you to rebound from a negative hit and inspire you to do the best you can. They help you to see the light at the end of the tunnel. Life is easier if you have people around you who give joy to your journey, who help you to speed up, who help you to rest, who help you to estimate which direction is the better one, who help you to let go of irrelevant things. Another positive aspect is the more you hang out with positive people and have a positive attitude, the more like-minded people you will attract. This is also relevant for your work colleagues.

Be the Person You Want to Be

One of the most eye-opening inspirations I have acquired was from the previously quoted book "The 7 Habits of Highly Effective People" by Steven Covey.

The second habit Stephen Covey covers in this book is "begin with the end in mind". To understand what he means by that, he encourages the reader to do a little experiment. Imagine you are at a funeral. All the seats are filled with people dressed in black. A casket sits at the front of the room. Imagine you can hear the eulogies being given to the person. Now imagine that your body is in that casket. It is your funeral. The people dressed in black are your friends and family members. He then tells the reader to ask the following, and in my opinion very powerful, question: "how do we want to be remembered?" How do you want people to describe you at the end? Are you shaping your personality and your way of life accordingly to how you want to be described? Are you living the life you want to live? Are you the person you want to be? Life is a choice. It is your life. Choose wisely and choose consciously.

Dr Bruce Lipton, an American developmental biologist, argued that 95% of our life is controlled by the subconscious mind. According to Dr Lipton, we are programmed to think and behave in a certain way – especially during the first seven years of our life, and through observations but also through what we hear we are programming our subconscious. If someone hears in their environment or from their family statements such as "things are hard", "you cannot make it", "life is a struggle", "who do you think you are", the person's programme will be like that. In other words, if you do not take control of your life, your life is being lived for you, even though you think you are living your life.

Based on Dr Lipton's idea, only 5% of the time in your life are you using your conscious mind, which is creative. The conscious mind is also the key for how you can influence the programme and put new programmes into your subconscious mind. As a first step, Dr Lipton suggests that you recognise where you struggle. With the help of the conscious mind, which can learn in many ways, you can help to overwrite certain programmes. The fundamental elements in doing so are simply repetition and practice. To illustrate this, just do the following exercise: smile for a minute. Even if you are faking the smile, it is tricking the brain and signals that you are happy, which then can activate the benefits of feeling happy, such as reducing stress, putting you at ease, and lowering your heart rate to name a few. If your subconscious always hears "I am happy" there will be a point when the subconscious understands "I am happy". Then you do not need to do it again. It will be automated.

Ultimately, it is your conscious decision that will dictate where you go with your life. You are the pilot of your life. Take it in your hands and get the best out of it. The best? Yes, the best. The best is what you think the best is for you. The best is that you go after your dreams. The best is not what society tells us it is. Society tells you to buy a house, have a new car and have a good paying job. Most people go for that. With the downside that their hopes and dreams fall short.

Life is too short to spend time and energy on things we actually do not want to do. Therefore, run after your dreams. It won't always be easy. It won't always be straightforward. It will certainly have many ups and downs, yet do not let the downs make you think of giving up. Believe in your dreams. Believe in yourself. Be a positive person and genuinely be interested in people and spread love. Hate and anger will not bring you much other than frustration and negative energy.

Many people are blocked by fear to fulfil their dreams. What would others think about me? What if it doesn't work out? Rather than focusing on what can go wrong, think about what can go right. Place your focus on what you want and get excited about the outcome. You need to take risk. Because it matters. You know why? Because it is about you and because life is not unlimited.

The Top Five Regrets of the Dying

Bronnie Ware, a former nurse, who spent several years working in palliative care, looking after and caring for patients in the last weeks of their lives, collected many regrets elderly people revealed just before they died. Inspired by her discovery, Mrs Ware wrote a book about her experiences called "The Top 5 Regrets of the Dying". Below are the top five regrets of the dying, as witnessed by Mrs Ware:

1. I wish I would have had the courage to live a life true to myself, not the life others expected of me.
2. I wish I hadn't worked so hard.
3. I wish I'd had the courage to express my feelings.
4. I wish I had stayed in touch with my friends.
5. I wish that I had let myself be happier.

You may be thinking "I have not even started my career and this guy is confronting me with funeral, casket and dying". It is not my intention to scare you. But after all, this will come. Or do you know any person who is immortal? It is now the time to take control of your life and live it as you want. Do not let society dictate how to live your life. Of course, we want to be accepted and it is easier to do the same thing that most other people are doing. It is always easier and safer in our comfort zone and people tend to stay there. Please just re-check the top regret.

Look out for Inspiration

I am always keen to talk to senior people and learn from their experience and from the life lessons they have. Most of the things elderly people share are as valuable today as they were then. Additionally, I am also interested in reading, and a couple of years ago I found this wonderful speech about life by Coca Cola's former CEO, Bryan Dyson. It was delivered at the 172nd commencement of the Georgia Tech Institute, on September 6, 1996. Below is the full text.

"Imagine life as a game in which you are juggling some five balls in the air. You name them work, family, health, friends, and spirit and you're keeping all of these in the air.

You will soon understand that 'work' is a rubber ball. If you drop it, it will bounce back. But the other four balls – family, health, friends, and spirit – are made of glass. If you drop one of these, they will be irrevocably scuffed, marked, nicked, damaged or even shattered. They will never be the same. You must understand that and strive for balance in your life.

How?

Don't undermine your worth by comparing yourself with others. It is because we are different that each of us is special.

Don't set your goals by what other people deem important. Only you know what is best for you.

Don't take for granted the things closest to your heart. Cling to them as you would your life, for without them, life is meaningless.

Don't let your life slip through your fingers by living in the past or for the future. By living your life one day at a time, you live ALL the days of your life.

Don't give up when you still have something to give. Nothing is really over until the moment you stop trying.

Don't be afraid to admit that you are less than perfect. It is this fragile thread that binds us to each other.

Don't be afraid to encounter risks. It is by taking chances that we learn how to be brave.

Don't shut love out of your life by saying it's impossible to find. The quickest way to receive love is to give it; the fastest way to lose love is to hold it too tightly: and the best way to keep love is to give it wings.

Don't run through life so fast that you forget not only where you've been, but also where you are going.

Don't forget, a person's greatest emotional need is to feel appreciated.

Don't be afraid to learn. Knowledge is weightless, a treasure you can always carry easily.

Don't use time or words carelessly. Neither can be retrieved.

Life is not a race, but a journey to be savoured each step of the way. Yesterday is history. Tomorrow is a Mystery and Today is a gift: that's why we call it 'The Present'."

Closing Comments

I hope that I have been able to stick to my promise and provide you with relevant and useful insights into the interview process and into business and help you to better prepare for your next upcoming job interview. Moreover, once you get the job, what to do in order to be successful.

While doing so, I also wanted to challenge you to really think about what matters for you the most in life. Will you be going with the flow and, like most people, give up on your dreams bit by bit? Will you be a member of the mainstream and eat what everyone else is eating, do what everyone else is doing, wear what everyone else is wearing and have the same opinion as everyone else.

I was 27 when I truly realised how the norm can influence your behaviour and limit your thinking. It was when I was backpacking in South America. I had plenty of time and wanted to discover Brazil after being in Venezuela. I took the plane from Caracas to Sao Paulo. Just before we landed at our destination, you could already feel some hecticness going through the plane. Some people were already collecting their hand luggage before the plane wheels had even touched the ground. Somehow, and unnecessarily, stress was created. People were rushing and for some it felt like they were running to their next destination. Automatically, a flow built up and the other passengers and I were caught in a mass of people going in the same direction, to the exit. Some were lucky as someone picked them up, others were grabbing a taxi, but as I was on budget travelling I went with the flow who were taking a bus to the city centre.

After few minutes of landing in Brazil, I ended up queueing in the line to buy a bus ride. On a big banner you could see the cost for a one-way ticket to the city centre. It was approximately $10. As I had many people in front of me I was checking the surroundings. I saw a man cleaning the street outside the terminal. I looked at him and I started to think. I thought about how much money this man would earn a month and questioned if he could afford to pay $20 each day to get to work and back home. I went outside and approached this man with my broken Portuguese. I asked him how to get to the city centre by bus. As I was a tourist, he instantly showed me the place where I was queueing before. I said to him that I wanted to know where he takes the bus. He got my point and showed me the public bus station, which was located just behind the terminal. I went there and, as I had assumed, I paid only $0,5 for the one-way ticket.

This experience was another eye-opener for me. It demonstrated to me how others can influence me. Many big companies, especially in the advertising industry, are aware of this and use it to their benefit in order to manipulate people. Think about your last visit to IKEA. What did you want to buy? And, what did you end up buying? Did you pass by all items that they sell, or could you directly go to the storage rack to pick up what you initially wanted to buy?

The point I want to make is that you should not allow others to think for you and make up your opinion. Every individual should think for themselves and live their own life. Time is limited, so do not waste it living others' life.

Ask yourself what you want. Ask yourself what the purpose of your life should be. Ask yourself what is important for you and find out your dream(s). What are the things you would regret if you cannot accomplish them?

Every now and then, you need to make decisions in life. What is important is that you do not look back and regret the decisions you have made. Have an action plan and be disciplined. And be true to yourself. Listen carefully to your gut and inner self. Your heart and soul will guide you, in the good and also in the hard times.

Money comes, and money goes. I have yet to witness a rich person taking all his wealth with him when he passes away. Do not give up things for being in a comfort zone and for money, and do not pursue a job just for the money. Find out what you are talented at. Everyone has a talent.

One of the quotes that has been imprinted in my mind is from Robert De Niro when in the movie "A Bronx Tale" his son asks him if he has talent and if he could be a baseball player. Here is Robert De Niro's answer:

 "You can be anything you want to be. Remember, the saddest thing in life is wasted talent. You could have all the talent in the world but if you don't do the right thing, then nothing happens."